SMALL DETAILS MAKE A BIG DIFFERENCE

Copyright ⓒ 2024 by CHANG SEIL.
Published by Bybooks, #1005, 23 Seonyu-ro 49-gil, Yeongdeungpo-gu, Seoul, Korea.
All rights reserved.
ISBN : 979-11-5877-372-4 03190

SMALL DETAILS MAKE A BIG DIFFERENCE

BY CHANG SEIL

ByBooks

I am thankful to have lessons to learn and share.
Nothing would mean more to me than my philosophy guiding
those who are lost, back to the right path.
That is the ultimate reason I wrote this book.

PROLOGUE

WHY SMALL DETAILS MATTER

I've been moving forward for 83 years. Anyone who has lived for 83 years is sure to have experienced ups and downs, twists and turns. Reflecting on a life lived, people often joke, "If I were to write about my life, I would end up writing several volumes." However, I have my own reason for wanting to write a book: I have the unique experience of having started from scratch and traveled the world to build a business.

The sky is most beautiful at two times of the day: sunrise and dusk. My sunrise was modest, yet I yearned for a splendid dusk. Just as today's happiness results from past efforts, a splendid evening can only follow the sweat poured out at midday. My noontimes were intense, and I made extraordinary efforts, always moving forward for the sake of my company, society, and nation. Now, at the dusk of my life, I am heeding the call from above to share my valuable experience and knowledge, instead of keeping it to myself. This is important because it's the least I can do for the world we share and fulfill my duty. The world is such a formidable battlefield that merely standing upright is a challenge. The experiences and knowledge of those who have endured are treasures, helping to navigate life for the better. I am thankful to have lessons to learn and share. Nothing would mean more to me than my philosophy guiding those who are lost, back to the right path. That is the ultimate reason I wrote this book.

Through my professional life, I've come to realize the importance of several things. The first is skill. Skill is the foundation, as having a job means you are a skilled professional in that field; thus, possessing the appropriate skill is fundamental. Only with the right skills can you meet your customers' needs satisfactorily.

Equally important are human relationships. Jobs rely on interpersonal connections. Some skilled individuals falter due to poor interpersonal relationships, while others with strong relationships fail due to a lack of skills. Success in your profession and recognition in your field come only when you excel in both areas.

To ascend in your professional life, developing superior skills and interpersonal relationships is essential. This book will candidly discuss the importance of these elements, drawn from my 57 years as an employee and entrepreneur. I've discovered a principle that can be distilled into one concept: small details. My philosophy is that attention to the minutest detail is crucial for building advanced skills, applicable not just in work but across all life aspects, including relationships and health.

I hope readers will uncover the value of little details and see how they are beneficial in their own lives. Moreover, if young people are inspired to chart the right course in life after reading this, my goal will be achieved.

Prologue
Why Small Details Matter 6

Chapter 1
Ilsung Embraces the World with Small Details

My Own Stage, Embracing the World

Establishing My Stage in a 59m² Office	18
The First Order for Facility Repair Work	21
Domestic Market is Too Small: Turn Your Attention to Overseas	24
Hamaca Project in Venezuela	30
Tapping the Uncharted Market in Iran	33
Jumping to the Top in the Race by Winning an Order from a Saudi Company	38
Flying to London to Deliver an Order to a Saudi Company	42
Pioneering the Chinese Market	46
The Meaning of Ilsung and Its Corporate Philosophy	50
A 200-fold Growth in 27 Years: From $1M Export to $200M Export	55
From a 59 m² Office to a 200 km² Factory	59
Glories of Ilsung: From Industrial Awards to the Gold Tower Order of Industrial Service Merit	63
The Localization of Petrochemical Plants is the Key!	66

Chapter 2

Small Details, the Drive Behind Growth

A Whole is Nothing But the Sum of Small Parts

The Reason Ilsung Drew the Attention of the World	74
SaDe Makes a Big Difference in Skills	80
SaDe begins with understanding the significance of even the smallest components within the whole!	85
SaDe is Everything: A Whole is the Sum of Its Smallest Details	88
Technical Achievements and Skills Achieved Through SaDe	92
SaDe Also Applies to Trusting Relationships!	95
The Law of SaDe Applies to All Fields	99

Chapter 3
The Origin of My Belief in SaDe

My Extraordinary Intuition Experience

Childhood Spent in Japan	108
On the Way Back to the Homeland After Liberation	111
Whole Family Sheltering in One Room in Daebong-dong, Daegu	115
The Korean War and the Discovery of Super Intuition Within Me	117
A Good Student With Top Grades	120
Downfall of the Family	124
Concerns Of the Eldest Son	127
The Grand Dream of a President and a Judge	131
Choosing Between the Korean Military Academy and Seoul National University College of Engineering	134
Why I Almost Threw Up After Eating Meat	138
Making Money as a Tutor While Studying in College	141

Chapter 4
SaDe Learned from Life

Lessons about Small Details

Applying for ROTC and the Training from Hell	148
Returning Home as a Commissioned Officer	152
First Military Service at the Army Signal School	155
Practical Experience Learned While Being Signal Commander for a Frontline Unit	159
One Month of Harsh Experience in My First Job	164
the Importance of Small Details Learned Through Life Experience	167
A Subordinate with Superior-Level Performance	171
Devotion to SaDe Builds Confidence and Skills	178
the Field is the Best Place to Learn SaDe	180
Supervising the Construction of Offshore Crude Oil Pipelines and Operation of Long-Distance Onshore Oil Pipelines	184
Changes in the Company and a Conflict of Choices	188

Chapter 5

Faith and Trust Built with SaDe

Crisis is the Best Opportunity to Build Faith

Competency Creates Faith in Your Ability	194
Crisis is a Golden Opportunity to Build Faith	199
A Sudden Health Crisis	203
Crisis Following the Sudden Terrorist Attacks of 9/11	208
Tearing up the contract with the Brazilian state-owned company	211
Non-Payment Crisis with a U.S. Company	213
KIKO Incident and Turning the Tables 10 Years Later	219
My First Experience of Jail	224
The Secret to Union-Free Management	228
Communication and Sharing: Keys to Trust!	231
Why the Industrial Peace Award Matters More to Me Than the Gold Tower Order of Industrial Service Merit	235

Chapter 6

SaDe for Health and Life-long Learning

Health is Also a Competency

Two-hour Barefoot Walk along a Mountain Trail Despite Being in My 80s	240
A Cold Bath in the Mountains in the Middle of Winter	243
Health Strengthened Through Exercise	245
Top Golf Skills	248
Learning to Ski and Quickly Becoming a skiing enthusiast	251
The Secret to SaDe Lies in Constant Study!	254
A Passion for Learning, Even in Old Age!	258
Dreaming of Corporate Social Contribution and Missionary Work	263
Little Memories of Life	266

Epilogue

For Those Preparing for the Second Half of Life! 271

CHAPTER 1

ILSUNG EMBRACES THE WORLD WITH SMALL DETAILS

MY OWN STAGE, EMBRACING THE WORLD

ESTABLISHING MY STAGE IN A 59m² OFFICE

In December 1983, four years into Chun Doo-hwan's new military regime, I stood facing the turbulent sea of Ulsan, the sharp cold wind assaulting my cheeks. My hands, buried in my pockets, found a piece of paper.

It was my resignation letter.

Imagine the trepidation of leaving a 19-year career. Yet, my resolve was unshakeable. I aimed to quit and build my own organization instead of being part of another's. I wanted to create a stage from which to engage with the world. This dream had been with me since joining Korea National Oil Corporation (KNOC), where I initially planned to learn for 10 years before founding my own enterprise at 35. Life, however, extended this tenure by nearly a decade.

I was in a situation where the urgency to act was undeniable. At the time, I was working for KNOC, a state-run petrochemical leader, yet it was mostly dependent on imports due to a lack of domestic technology. I believed in my ability to achieve self-sufficiency if only I was given a chance, and I was confronted with a decisive moment.

The following year, 1984, became a monumental one for me; that was when I left my job of 19 years to start my own company. Starting a company requires capital, and all I had was about $70,000 in severance pay. It was a considerable sum then, but far from enough to establish the oil plant company I envisioned. Starting an oil plant business required much more due to the necessity of a large factory and equipment.

Nevertheless, I opted to begin the business with just half of my funds, reserving the remainder as a safety net. Being single might have simplified things, but I had a family to support. While employment guarantees a stable income, running your own business does not. I had to ensure my family's financial stability, which could be jeopardized by an unsteady income. Moreover, entrepreneurship is fraught with risks, necessitating an emergency fund for unforeseen circumstances.

I shared my plans with my wife, who understandably objected. However, my determination was unwavering. To balance my obligations to my family and new company, I leased a small 59m2 office in Suam-dong, Nam-gu, Ulsan, and hired three employees, using only half of my savings. At that time, I was already in my mid-40s—a late start by any standards, demanding that I work much harder to compensate. My late entry meant that I had to accelerate the growth of my business without the advantages of substantial capital, a large business, or many employees.

At first, I aimed for 'stable growth' rather than taking risks. Instead of overextending myself financially, I started small, securing modest contracts like facility repairs by leveraging my knowledge and experience. I planned to save money from these projects before considering any expansion. However, frustratingly, I didn't receive any orders for the first few months.

I encountered fear like never before. While at the oil company, I managed monthly payments of $5 million. But now, I fretted over a few thousand dollars for office rent and employee salaries. The fear was palpable—I knew I would incur significant losses if the situation persisted. I felt like a tiny leaf adrift in an immense sea.

THE FIRST ORDER FOR FACILITY REPAIR WORK

No orders were coming in, despite the open door. My office was decently staffed with a female bookkeeper and male employees, but there had been no business for months. Initially, I feigned indifference, hoping for an order at any moment. However, maintaining this pretense became increasingly difficult. Whispers among the employees grew, fueled by fears of imminent business failure. Recognizing their concern mirrored my own, I knew I needed to regain composure.

Then, a phone call from my former company broke the silence. They had a plant machinery maintenance project and inquired if I could take it on. It wasn't large, but it was my first order, and I accepted without hesitation. Yet, a challenge presented itself: my experience at the oil company was managerial, and I lacked specific knowledge about on-site maintenance.

Nevertheless, I've always had an intuitive knack for problem-solving. An idea struck me, and I promptly consulted with field experts, rapidly assimilating the necessary know-how, perhaps even surpassing the experts. The project was not only completed smoothly but also under budget.

The first project's profit margin exceeded 30%, covering office rent and employee salaries for six months—a substantial relief. More orders began to flow in. With each new project, I invested time to learn every aspect to execute the job with expertise, building a reputation for reliability.

About three months into my venture, a significant opportunity arose. Yeongnam Chemical needed to construct a new sulfuric acid tank after their previous one corroded. It was a big project, probably costing hundreds of thousands of dollars. Despite its scale and the likelihood of established companies bidding, Ilsung, with its brief history of only three months, entered the fray. It was a veritable David versus Goliath scenario, but I had confidence.

Before bidding, I scrutinized the estimate dozens of times. Given it was well over a hundred thousand dollars, any excessive estimation could result in a failed bid. Despite my extensive experience drafting estimates at the oil company, the prospect of handling an order worth hundreds of thousands left me nervous. I cautiously submitted a construction estimate of $130,000 and, to my astonishment, Ilsung was chosen for the job. It seemed divine providence had favored my company in the competitive bid.

Drawing on my past experience and knowledge, I managed the project diligently. Thankfully, the civil service department head, familiar with my solid reputation at the oil company, offered his full cooperation and support. This collaborative environment was invaluable. I meticulously calculated the sulfuric acid tank's steel plate thickness and visited the site three times daily to ensure every detail was perfect. The project yielded a 30% profit margin, providing substantial funds for business expansion and bringing me closer to realizing the dream of building my own factory.

DOMESTIC MARKET IS TOO SMALL: TURN YOUR ATTENTION TO OVERSEAS

THE FIRST ORDER FROM OVERSEAS AND AN ORDER FROM FLUOR

Luck was on my side, as I found myself searching for a factory site less than a year after establishing my company. The increasing volume of orders highlighted the necessity of owning a facility where I could process them all. By chance, a factory in Yeonam-dong, near Ulsan Airport, was up for auction. Despite being on sloped ground with restrictive access, the 1,650m² space was a significant upgrade from a 59m² office. Priced at $130,000, it was a financial stretch, but I managed to secure it with a deferred payment agreement. I dedicated myself to everything from repairs to factory construction and even tackled sales and fieldwork. Following this, Ilsung's growth surged, with a 200% average annual increase. By 1991, we were honored with the Industrial Peace Award, acknowledging our exceptional labor-management relations. It was a great honor to get the award, because it seemed that my years of hardwork was being recognized.

Our reputation solidified through partnerships with conglomerates like Daelim Industrial, SK E&C, LG E&C, and Hyundai Heavy Industries. Recognition from these industry giants bolstered my confidence. It was around this time that supplies from Japan's Mitsubishi Heavy Industries arrived, and it became my first international order. This success made the domestic market seem limited and spurred my ambition to expand globally.

At that time, my eldest son, fresh from his studies in the United States, was working at Ilsung as a manager. Despite his degree in commerce, he showed little interest in our industry and was considering other career options. Contrary to his views, I believed that his American experience could complement our aspirations to enter international markets and create great results. It seemed he was thinking along the same lines; one day, he expressed a desire to help Ilsung break into overseas markets before possibly moving on. Overjoyed, I immediately entrusted my US-educated son with the task.

My son started identifying global companies, leveraging his overseas exposure and English proficiency to target not just Japan but also Europe and America. During this initiative, we noticed projects from the US-based Fluor and Saudi Arabia's Yanbu. Fluor, impressed by Ilsung's dealings with Mitsubishi Heavy Industries, approached us first for a collaboration, despite our relatively small profile on the global stage.

My son, along with an Ilsung engineer, boarded a plane to the

Machines (left) and products (right) from the first factory in Yeonam-dong, Ulsan, that I acquired at auction.

United States. They headed to southern California, where Fluor was located. It was near the University of Southern California, where my son had studied and an area familiar to him from his study days. In LA, he met with Fluor's staff, who, as he perceived, seemed somewhat dismissive of Ilsung, a smaller and lesser-known entity compared to Fluor. He had prepared a 26-item presentation, but by noon, they had only discussed two items due to the staff's meticulousness. Soon it was lunch time, and my son was having a sandwich with soda, feeling disheartened by the morning meeting that hadn't seemed to go so well. While he was having his lunch, he was approached by an Indian-American chief engineer from Fluor. He asked my son where he was staying, and my son told him somewhere in downtown LA. Hearing my son, the engineer was intrigued by my son's familiarity with LA. Upon learning of my son's alma mater, the engineer revealed he was an alumnus from the same college, having graduated a few years before my son.

Weighed down by the task of presenting the remaining 24 items, my son was about to resume when the chief engineer encouraged him to relax. Over the next two hours, the engineer personally approved all 24 items. It was the moment when the formidable network of the University of Southern California alumni truly came through. After the presentation, my son told the engineer, "I've crossed the Pacific to make this presentation. I wish I had more than one package to present to you in this trip." Upon hearing this, the engineer made a few phone calls and found out that there was a stainless-steel package. He asked my son if he could also handle the stainless-steel package. Without hesitation, my son answered, "Of course!" He accepted the order, which was double the size of the initial one, before triumphantly returning with orders totaling three million dollars instead of just the one million he had originally aimed for.

Following this success, Ilsung executed the first order flawlessly, establishing an ongoing relationship with Fluor. My son and I made frequent visits to Fluor in America, where our connections through the University of Southern California alumni network proved invaluable. This rapport eventually led Ilsung to secure consecutive orders for the Irving Project and a Saudi Arabian Project via Fluor.

At that time, air travel to the United States was not as efficient as it is today: flights were longer and the planes experienced more severe turbulence. I often arrived in the US exhausted. Jet lag left me sleepy during the day and restless at night, which was troubling. I feared that sleep deprivation would compromise my health and jeopardize important business meetings, which were usually scheduled for early mornings. Given America's vast size, it sometimes took over an hour's drive to reach a company. I still believe that enduring these hidden hardships was key to Ilsung's success in penetrating the U.S. market.

I made particular efforts to bond with Fluor's lead engineer, who was my contemporary. I even hosted a party for him and his team at Long Beach. Our relationship evolved into one of trust, and he continued to allocate projects to Ilsung, which helped us expand our business internationally.

HAMACA PROJECT IN VENEZUELA
THE FIRST BIG ORDER

There was news that Fluor was moving its headquarters from Long Beach to Aliso Viejo, further south. I visited the new location several times to maintain close contact with the lead engineer. During my visits, I learned from the engineer that there was a substantial construction order for a large-scale petrochemical plant in Venezuela, named the Hamaca project. It entailed building a facility with special technology for high-temperature and high-pressure oil refining. Confident in Ilsung's capabilities to handle the construction, I submitted a bid. I coveted the project due to its scale, which was larger than any project I had undertaken thus far. At that time, Ilsung's annual sales were about $2.5 million, and this project alone could surpass tens of millions of dollars.

In pursuit of securing the order, I cultivated a relationship with the lead engineer, who had the decision-making authority for the project. I would dine with him and bring simple souvenirs during my visits, which made him increasingly fond of me.

Contrary to the belief that all crude oils are similar, their properties vary significantly by source. Some, like those involved in the Hamaca project, are denser and require higher refining pressures. This necessitated thicker and stronger steel plates for the factory equipment. Ilsung's bid was successful, and we leveraged our technological expertise to deliver high-quality products ahead of schedule. Additionally, we conducted an extra inspection post-construction with two employees, despite no request from the engineer.

The construction was a great success. The Hamaca project was a major order valued at $37 million, providing Ilsung an opportunity to have its technological prowess recognized because we successfully delivered high-temperature, high-pressure products made of special materials. In the spring of 2023, during a visit to Fluor in the U.S., someone from the company thanked me, noting that the products supplied by Ilsung were still performing well at the Venezuelan plant. I felt a deep sense of pride for Ilsung.

Even after the project's completion, I maintained a good relationship with the lead engineer, staying in contact and visiting him occasionally. Then, I learned that he—suffering from a bad heart condition—had undergone surgery to replace his artificial heart, which had a lifespan of 10 years. I was deeply concerned and hoped for a swift recovery. Unfortunately, his prognosis was poor, and his condition worsened until I received the sad news of his passing. It hit me hard, as I felt like I had lost an old friend. Why do good people always seem to die young? This question remains a mystery to me.

Meanwhile, my eldest son, who played a significant role in Ilsung's initial expansion into international markets, informed me that he had contributed his part to the company and decided to take a short leave to pursue an MBA in the United States. His departure was bittersweet; I was proud, but also sad to see him go. After years, he returned to Ilsung and now serves as the CEO.

TAPPING THE UNCHARTED MARKET IN IRAN

Ilsung has made inroads into several international markets, and Iran is one of them. Historically, large corporations from the United States and Europe avoided seeking orders from Iran due to national sentiments against Western culture. Korean companies were no exception, but I was determined to explore opportunities within the Iranian market. Our break came when we received an inquiry from a company called Ajaram, which was interested in purchasing some equipment from us. My employees thought we should refuse the order. They argued that the order was only for parts, not a whole plant, and it was too small. Besides, it was too risky, since no one else was doing business in Iran. But I believed in taking the chance to establish a presence in any new market, whether in Iran or elsewhere.

To assess the situation, I dispatched a few employees to Iran for preliminary business discussions. Upon their return, they expressed skepticism about securing orders. Undeterred, I took the initiative to travel to Iran myself. During my visit, I observed the country's dynamics under the leadership of Ruhollah Khomeini, who had replaced the pro-American Pahlavi dynasty with an Islamic Republic through a revolution. Khomeini's expulsion of Western influences, advocacy for Islamic fundamentalism, and establishment of a theocracy, left Iran in a state that was neither democratic nor communist.

This national atmosphere inevitably impacts business operations. At the time, corporate culture was predominantly built on a strict hierarchy. However, in Iranian companies, there was an environment where superiors needed to be mindful of their subordinates' opinions. For instance, in an Iranian company meeting with six participants, if the team leader attempts to make a unilateral decision, a subordinate might protest to higher-ups that the leader is making arbitrary company decisions. This culture prevented even team leaders from making decisions independently for fear of backlash. Ever since my youth, I have had the intuition to recognize problems during crises. Upon arriving in Iran and meeting with their team, my intuition proved insightful, and I grasped this dynamic.

In such an environment, it's challenging for a chief engineer to make sound decisions. I reached out to one employee who seemed insightful during the meeting, offering advice on resolving their issue. I explained that their approach might further complicate an already complex situation and advised him on a solution. I encouraged him to consult with me anytime he faced difficulties. This ap-

Ilsung became the first Korean company to win a $13 million order from Iran.

proach likely built trust, as they began seeking my advice on various issues. As a result of the guidance I provided and the trust it fostered, Ilsung secured its first order in Iran, marking a milestone as the first Korean company to do so.

There was an incident even after the decision had been finalized. The president of the Iranian company requested a meeting with me. When I inquired about the agenda, he mentioned a reservation at a high-end Indian restaurant and proposed discussing the matter post-meal. Although his approach was aggravating, insisting on dining before discussing, I reluctantly agreed. After the meal, we returned to his office where he dismissed the staff, secured privacy, and requested a 10% discount on our agreed order—a proposition I could not entertain as the terms were already settled. In response to my refusal, he became desperate, imploring on his knees for a concession. After a protracted two-hour debate, I excused myself, citing a need for the restroom. Outside, I approached a company executive and asked him what was going on. He told me that he thought his boss was having a fight with me inside his office, before clarifying the president's predicament. According to him, the president had almost nothing important to do, and he could save face only if he could get a discount on the order. With this insight, I returned and, feigning capitulation, proposed a 2% discount. The president pushed for more generosity, and we eventually settled on a 4% discount, to which he jubilantly responded with a thumbs-up, exclaiming, "You win!" That's how Ilsung successfully signed its first contract with an Iranian firm.

Once, I arrived at the airport at 10:00 PM and encountered difficulties after being stopped by airport security. The guard, upon seeing my passport, halted me to inquire if I was acquainted with a Mr. Chang, who allegedly had deceived security and caused trouble sometime in the past. I found myself implicated simply because I shared the same surname, Chang. The guard seemed to presume that sharing a surname indicated familial relations. I assured him I did not know this individual, but my words didn't convince him. He took my passport and directed me to retrieve it from the immigration office the following day. Confused, I reached out to an Ajaram employee for assistance, but he did not answer. I later learned that he had deliberately avoided the call, fearing company involvement. With no alternative, I spent the night without my passport and only regained possession of it the next day.

My passport caused another incident at an Iranian airport. I was detained by security because my passport contained numerous U.S. entry stamps, leading the Iranian intelligence agency to suspect me as a U.S. Central Intelligence Agency operative. It almost resulted in a denial of my entry. With the assistance of local Koreans and the Korean Ministry of Foreign Affairs, I narrowly avoided this crisis, but it was nonetheless, a harrowing ordeal.

As I traveled to Iran frequently and developed a relationship of trust, everyone at the Iranian company started to like me. They even took me around and showed me their facilities. I toured companies in Tehran, observed their facilities, held meetings with them, and provided them with advice. I also toured factory facilities located in a place called Arak, which was about a four-hour drive from Tehran. The area was home to several factories producing weapons. They invited me to their home, served me a meal, and provided me with a place to sleep. In return, I did not hesitate to offer them advice, drawing upon all of my past experience and knowledge.

Iran's companies were state-owned and had as many facilities as Hyundai Heavy Industries in Korea, but many of them were underused. So, I advised them on how to make the best use of these facilities, and it resulted in an unexpected outcome: They proposed giving the business rights to Ilsung. As a result, Ilsung was able to secure an order worth a whopping $13 million by pioneering the Iranian market. What initially seemed like a small-scale order of parts ended up snowballing into a massive order.

JUMPING TO THE TOP IN THE RACE BY WINNING AN ORDER FROM A SAUDI COMPANY

Once, we submitted an estimate to SABIC, a state-owned Saudi petrochemical company. It turned out that Ilsung was just one of the six companies that submitted bids to win the order, but Ilsung quoted the highest estimate among them. Having the highest estimate meant that Ilsung was the least likely to win the order.

However, I am not the type of person who gives up easily. I flew to Singapore right away. When I met with the person in charge, Ilsung had been completely excluded from the list of likely candidates to win the order. That was expected, and I was told to give up because it was too little too late. But I examined the situation and resubmitted a bid with an adjusted estimate. I also met with the chief engineer, trying to build a close relationship with him. At first, my approach was met with an unenthusiastic response, but as time passed, he noticed how sincere I was. I flew to Singapore several more times and continued to build a relationship with the chief engineer. Soon, the Chief Engineer began to trust me, and Ilsung eventually won the order. At that time, the adjusted estimate I submitted and the trust relationship with the chief engineer played a big role, and I couldn't help but say that it was a great achievement that brought Ilsung from last in the race to the forefront.

After this incident, rival companies would make a self-deprecatory remark that once Chang Seil joins the race, everyone else should just give up hope. That's how thorough and persistent I was in my efforts. I refused to give up as far as my business went. I think this is the core of entrepreneurship. Usually, people give up when something seems a little difficult. Nothing can be accomplished with that kind of attitude.

In the Bible, there is a story about four men who enter through the roof to meet Jesus and have a paralyzed man healed. The situation at the time was that they had little hope of entering the house where Jesus was staying because people were flocking to the house in droves to be healed by Jesus. But those four men refused to give up. They knew they could not enter the house from the traditional ground access openings, so they came up with the idea of breaking into the house from the roof. How were they able to come up with such a brilliant idea?

I believe this is a result of differences in beliefs. They were able to come up with an idea that made the impossible possible because they had faith that they would definitely be healed by Jesus. Similarly, I have faith and confidence that I can achieve anything, which is why I don't give up on anything. Of course, belief and confidence in one's work must be founded upon and supported by skills. I was able to overcome any challenge like a bulldozer, never giving up, all because I have faith in my abilities.

From the very beginning, I aimed for "stable growth"
rather than taking risks. However, as the business stabilized
and started to grow, I began to look overseas because
I felt that the domestic market was limited. I was able to tackle
any challenge with determination, all because I had faith in my abilities.

FLYING TO LONDON TO DELIVER AN ORDER TO A SAUDI COMPANY

People often say that a brave man wins a beautiful woman; I believe this applies equally to finding business opportunities. I tend to push forward courageously in business dealings. Once, I learned that a Saudi friend, whom I had met on a business trip to Saudi Arabia, was visiting Daerim in Korea. I immediately obtained my friend's phone number and contacted him. I seized this opportunity to promote our company, Ilsung, to Saudi companies by providing him with information about Ilsung. Subsequently, I flew to the Saudi headquarters to negotiate a business deal.

Upon arriving at the Saudi company, I discovered that an American company was also involved. They had already discussed the business deal with the Saudi company and were about to close the deal. It was apparent who would likely get the order. However, even in this situation, I refused to give up. First, we met with the person in

I flew to London to meet the project manager of a Saudi company and secured an order.

charge to understand the facts. Instead of merely pushing my own argument, I strived to make appropriate adjustments that fit the current situation. To achieve this, I considered the position of the person in charge from his perspective and then gradually expressed my own position. When building a relationship with another person, we should never view it as a one-time deal. Holding this belief, I flew to Saudi Arabia three times, making repeated efforts to establish a good relationship with the person in charge. Through these endeavors, I eventually succeeded in winning an order from the Saudi company.

SECURING A MAJOR BUSINESS DEAL WITH SABIC

Ilsung had numerous business interactions with Saudi companies, but our most significant client was SABIC, the Saudi company I mentioned earlier. When I first flew to Saudi Arabia with my eldest son to initiate business with this company, we learned that the managing director of SABIC (a Saudi Arabian) was in London. He was the chief manager of the project we were aiming to secure. Moreover, we discovered that the engineer in charge of the project was also in London. Realizing that it was the engineer, not the managing director, who held the real power, I immediately flew to London with my eldest son to meet with the engineer.

We arrived in London on a dark night and took a taxi to the engineer's location, which turned out to be quite a distance. The journey took an astonishing two hours, leading us to a rural area on the outskirts of London. The taxi driver remarked that he had never driven anyone such a long distance before, which was understandable given the notoriously high taxi fares in London.

The engineer was visibly surprised to see us arrive so late at night, incurring such an expensive taxi fare. His surprise soon turned to admiration for our dedication, and he expressed interest, suggesting that with our level of passion, he could trust us with the job. Thanks to these efforts, Ilsung successfully secured an order from SABIC.

Ilsung has this special knack for securing successive orders once they begin doing business with a client. Of course, Ilsung could achieve this because the company possesses top-notch technology and keeps its promise of delivering the highest-quality products right on time. Subsequently, Ilsung continued to receive second and third orders from SABIC, which also helped the company expand its business to the United States and Japan.

PIONEERING THE CHINESE MARKET

Around 2004, Ilsung was engaged in a number of construction projects for Taekwang Industries. Taekwang planned to build a factory in China to produce spandex fabric, and the managing director in charge of the project reached out to me for consultation. The year 2004 marked a period when China opened its doors, and Korean companies were entering the Chinese market in droves. When the managing director contacted me regarding the project, I was inwardly thrilled, perceiving it as a tremendous opportunity to penetrate the Chinese market.

In fact, I had been exploring the Chinese market for ten years, starting in 1994. At that time, Korea had just established diplomatic relations with China, and not many Korean companies were venturing into the Chinese market. I once had the opportunity to tour large cities in China with the chairman of Dongnam IP and noticed that most of the factories were rusty and in a dilapidated state. It was hard to imagine how anyone could work in such conditions. Korea's GS Caltex was constructing its own factories in Qingdao, Lidong, south of Qingdao. I attempted to participate in the construction of these factories, but budget issues prevented me from doing so. Consequently, Ilsung only supplied a few units of equipment.

Since I had memories of these experiences, I thought the Taekwang project was good news and began to actively work on it. However, the director of the Chinese civil service in charge presented a hurdle, as he informed us that a construction license was required to carry on with the project. This was really disappointing because, at the time, Ilsung did not possess a construction license. Realizing that I had to overcome this hurdle before I could enter China—a country built on a communist state system, even though the door was open—I started inquiring about how to obtain a construction license. Then, I found out that it took as long as a year to obtain one. This was not acceptable.

In the end, I had no choice but to find a solution through the Chinese director in charge. Using my good people skills, I approached him and succeeded in winning his heart. He advised me that I could open a consulting company to get the license faster. However, I had to prepare files that amounted to about 1,000 pages to open a consulting company. The Chinese director even personally came to the hotel where I was staying and had an employee stay with me to help me prepare these files, a process that took a week. Thanks to his help, I was able to prepare the document and open a consulting company. Soon after, I obtained the construction license, and Ilsung could start its construction business. This experience made me realize the importance of human relationships all over again.

Since we could not build a factory in China with our own personnel, we had to hire Chinese subcontractors. For our part, we only needed to send a few employees as supervisors. At the time, my Chinese was limited to what I'd learned from a conversational Chinese book I read on an airplane, but miraculously, I managed to meticulously select companies specializing in fields such as civil engineering, oil structures, machinery, and electrical instrumentation. The selection of a subcontractor is so crucial that the success or failure of a project often depends on it. Looking back, I am amazed at how I was able to interview companies, receive bids, and select them with my limited Chinese. It is incredibly challenging to select a company when you don't have sufficient language skills for effective communication. It was a real task to get the job done while working with many subcontractors from different backgrounds, such as an electrical company from Suzhou, a civil engineering and steel structure company from Shanghai, and a plumbing company from Hangzhou. However, I still believe that Ilsung managed the situation well, all thanks to divine grace.

The factory was scheduled to be built at a site in Changshu, a city near the Yangtze River, over three hours' drive from Shanghai.

The city had a population of 1.7 million. In China, most cities had populations almost equivalent to the large cities in Korea. The construction period was about eight months, and Ilsung's role at this time was to manage and supervise the entire construction process. Since our Chinese subcontractors were headquartered in Hangzhou and Suzhou, I frequently traveled to these cities to offer my consulting services. I also earned a significant amount of money from commissions.

Once, a Chinese government official asked me if I knew how to play golf. He mentioned that he played golf and was fairly good at it. So, we decided to play golf together. However, it turned out that he was just a beginner and hadn't really played golf before. His attempts to hit the ball made me laugh so hard, as he kept swinging and never came near the ball. We also went to a sauna together, and I remember being shocked at the sight of the floor, which was covered with a lot of dirt. Afterwards, I visited China more than 50 times to explore the Chinese market.

THE MEANING OF ILSUNG AND ITS CORPORATE PHILOSOPHY

When establishing a company, two key considerations are the company name and corporate philosophy. I believed that the names Samsung, Hyundai, and LG (Lucky Goldstar) played a significant role in their ascent to becoming top-tier companies. Therefore, I pondered deeply when tasked with naming the company I was about to establish. Like anyone with great ambition, I aspired to reach heights as vast as the world and even the universe. While observing the numerous stars and the sun in the sky, I naturally came up with the idea of combining 'sun' (Il) and 'stars' (Sung) for the company name. I was confident that nothing could be more wonderful than nurturing a company with an ambition burning like the sun and destined to shine brilliantly like the stars. This inspiration led to the name Ilsung.

The company was initially named Ilsung Industry when it was

founded in March 1984, but it was later renamed Ilsung Engineering. A second name change occurred in January 2007 to Ilsung Co., Ltd., under which the company reached its business peak. Subsequently, the company faced a series of crises until it underwent a third name change to Ilsung Hisco in January 2017, a name it retains to this day.

The next consideration was the corporate philosophy. Starting a venture without a clear philosophy can lead to a loss of direction and poor performance. Particularly in entrepreneurship, beginning without a solid philosophical foundation is akin to starting with a significant flaw. Since founding Ilsung, my vision has been to cultivate a company that thrives on trust. I believe that a company can only grow when it is built upon that most important element. This raises the question: how does one earn trust? In business terms, it involves possessing the skills to satisfy clients and, more importantly, maintaining honesty and keeping promises. I have adhered to this principle throughout my management of the company.

Furthermore, I recognized the importance of trust in human relationships. For a business owner, building relationships with partners is crucial, but so is fostering relationships with employees. A company can only continue to grow under the leadership of an owner who earns the employees' trust. Achieving this requires that you consider everything from the employees' perspective. Based on these reflections, I established the following motto for Ilsung:

'Ensure a prosperous life for those who work'
'Find and take responsibility for your own work'
'Operate democratically and autonomously'

In general, company mottos are often crafted from the management's perspective. However, I chose to create Ilsung's motto by thoroughly considering the employees' viewpoint. I believed this was the only way to truly earn their trust. The motto, 'Ensure a prosperous life for those who work', emerged from this perspective. Consequently, I endeavored to treat my employees exceptionally well and prioritized their welfare. Ilsung's reputation for its no labor union management is a result of our steadfast adherence to this motto.

Many might think that adequate compensation and benefits are sufficient for employee satisfaction, but fostering a sense of accomplishment in their work is equally vital. This approach builds employees' trust in the company. To achieve this sense of accomplishment, efficiency and a system of autonomy and responsibility are crucial. Mandating work leads to mechanical output and reduced efficiency. My time at the oil company, influenced by the US-based Gulf Oil Corporation, taught me the value of autonomy. The company's free atmosphere, rare during those authoritarian times, resonated with me and inspired me to implement a similar culture at Ilsung.

Creating a company motto required careful consideration and

extensive research. Finally, I established 'Find and take responsibility for your own work' and 'Operate in a democratic and autonomous manner.' Thanks to these mottos, Ilsung developed an organizational system where employees worked efficiently like a well-oiled machine, even with minimal management intervention. Additionally, principles of 'empathetic management'—where labor respects management and management trusts labor—and 'open management'—where all members share in the company's tasks—were realized. These principles have undeniably contributed to Ilsung's successful no labor union management.

I aspired to reach heights as vast as the world and even the universe.
While observing the countless stars and the sun in the sky,
I naturally came up with the idea of combining 'sun' (Il) and
'stars' (Sung) for the company name. I was confident that nothing
could be more wonderful than nurturing a company with an ambition
burning like the sun and destined to shine brilliantly, like the stars.
This inspiration led to the name Ilsung.

A 200-FOLD GROWTH IN 27 YEARS: FROM $1M EXPORT TO $200M EXPORT

As a result of diligent efforts and extensive global outreach, Ilsung achieved a $200M export milestone in 2010. This was a remarkable feat, considering the company's humble beginnings in a small office, initially taking modest facility repair orders from the Korea National Oil Corporation.

Ilsung evolved into a premier petrochemical plant production company, skilled in manufacturing a wide range of equipment including heat exchangers, pressure vessels, towers, condensers, reactors, fuel gas steam generators, heating furnaces, and modules for use in petrochemical and chemical plants, as well as oil field development. The company now boasts a 200 km2 factory facility, rivaling major corporations in scale. Its clientele includes global engineering giants like Bechtel, Shell, ExxonMobil, Technip, JGC, Chiyoda, Fluor, Stone & Webster, and others, with orders spanning over 20

November 30, 2010
Ilsung was honored with the Gold Tower Order of Industrial Service Merit by President Lee Myung-bak at the 47th Trade Day event.

countries across Southeast Asia, Africa, Latin America, and North America.

Technologically, Ilsung has achieved significant milestones. The company holds international certification codes including ASME CodeU, U2, U3, S, PP, N, NA, NPT, NS STAMP manufacturer qualifications, and the ISO 9001 quality certificate issued by HSB. Additionally, Ilsung gained international recognition with the OSHAS 18001 certification and a Special Equipment License from the China Ministry of Labor. The company also received ISO 14001 and ISO 18001 certifications from the Korea Gas Safety Corporation, underscoring its technological prowess in the gas sector. Beyond hardware technology, Ilsung has made strides in software technology as well. A notable example is the introduction of the ERP business computerization system in Korea, a pioneering step in integrating and managing all business processes from production to

December 15, 2008
I had the privilege of being invited to the Blue House to lunch with President Lee Myung-bak and other business leaders.

materials, equipment, outsourcing, budget, and accounts receivable and payable.

Ilsung initially focused on domestic sales, but in the early 1990s, it shifted towards exports, making its first significant overseas impact by exporting $1 million in 1993. The company's growth continued, capturing global attention when its export volume exceeded $100 million in 2007. In 2010, during a global economic recession following the 2008 financial crisis, Ilsung notably achieved exports of $200 million, a 50% increase from the previous year. This was particularly remarkable given the broader economic challenges, especially in exporting industries. Ilsung's export growth from $1 million in 1993 to $200 million in 2010, a 200-fold increase over 27 years, was an extraordinary feat that surprised the world.

Ilsung's achievements were globally recognized. In 2009, I was honored as the Trader of the Year who glorified Korea. The follow-

On January 20, 2009, during U.S. President Obama's inauguration reception

ing year, I received the Gold Tower Order of Industrial Service Merit from President Lee Myung-bak at the 47th Trade Day ceremony held at COEX in Samseong-dong, Seoul.

FROM A 59 M² OFFICE TO A 200 KM² FACTORY

Ilsung's growth mirrors its expanding facilities. Our first factory, acquired in 1984, spanned approximately 1,600 m². Located on a narrow road and built on sloping ground, it was modest and somewhat shabby. We operated there until 1989, when business growth necessitated a larger space.

By the end of 1989, Ilsung had moved to an 8,200 m² facility in Hwasan-ri, within the Onsan Industrial Complex in southern Ulsan. This marked the beginning of rapid expansion, both for the company and its manufacturing capabilities. Shortly after settling into the new 8,200 m² site, we acquired an additional 8,200 m² across the street to accommodate increasing demands. However, these facilities soon proved insufficient for the growing influx of supplies. Consequently, within just two to three years, we expanded further, acquiring factories #3, #4, and #5 in the vicinity.

The completion ceremony of the factory in Hwasan-ri, Ulsan, and the appearance of the headquarters building were celebrated on January 6, 1990.

An aerial view of the Ilsung factory, taken from an unmanned helicopter, was captured on May 15, 2009.

At that time, I was brimming with confidence, believing I could accomplish anything. Indeed, anyone would have felt a surge in confidence after achieving such success, and I was no exception. As I contemplated Ilsung's future, I became somewhat overzealous and began searching for a site to purchase in Ijin-ri, located on the beach within the Onsan Industrial Complex. Since Ilsung was an export company and shipped orders by ocean, I reasoned that building a factory near the beach was strategic. After personally visiting many potential sites, I decided to purchase a vast 132,000 m² plot (including both land and sea) in Ijin-ri. I believe it was around 1998. However, this decision turned out to be a nightmare. I had to sell the lot shortly after to cover losses incurred from a non-payment issue with a company in Kentucky, USA. It was heart-wrenching, to say the least. Although my dream of building a beachside factory ended in disappointment, it couldn't halt Ilsung's growth. People say dreams come true, and indeed, Ilsung's dream of an expanded factory was materializing, albeit in a different form.

In the 2000s, Ilsung could no longer manage all orders with our existing facilities, prompting a move to a larger 60,000 m² factory in Wonsan-ri, within the Onsan Industrial Complex, where Ilsung is currently based. Even then, the company continued its remarkable growth, necessitating further expansion of the factory facilities. Soon, the existing facilities were insufficient, leading Ilsung to acquire an additional 72,000 m² site and later another 50,000 m². These expansions began in the early 2000s, peaked in 2006, and were completed by 2008, by which time the total factory area spanned nearly 200,000 m². This scale is comparable to that of Hyundai Heavy Industries' factory site in the Onsan Industrial Complex. At this size, a morning round of the factory would take between an hour and a half to two hours.

Ilsung began in a modest 59 m² office and eventually acquired its first factory on a 1,600 m² site, growing into a massive company with facilities spread over 200,000 m². This history stirs my heart, symbolizing the growth and development akin to a child maturing over the years.

GLORIES OF ILSUNG: FROM INDUSTRIAL AWARDS TO THE GOLD TOWER ORDER OF INDUSTRIAL SERVICE MERIT

An ancient wise man once said, "Do your best and leave the results to heaven." What sound advice that was. I did my best and entrusted the outcomes to heaven, which graciously rewarded me with favorable results. Ilsung's development seemed like a divine gift, and I personally received numerous accolades.

Over the past 30 years, the company and I have been honored with many awards and medals. These include the Gyeongnam Industrial Peace Award; CEO of the Year Award; Industrial Peace Industry Award; Global Management Award; Presidential Citation; Business Leader of the Year Award; Special Achievement Award for the 60th Anniversary of the National Foundation; Trader of the Year who Glorified Korea Award; National Exemplary Small Businessman Award; Proud New Korean Award; Outstanding Labor-Management Relationship Company Award; and the Golden Tower

Order of Industrial Service Merit, to name just a few.

Among these, the Gyeongnam Industrial Peace Award I received in 1991 is particularly memorable because Go Hyun-jung, a popular actress at the time, interviewed me during the ceremony. Another significant accolade was the Presidential Citation I received in 1995 during the Kim Young-sam administration for my contributions to national industrial development. I also vividly remember the letter from President Kim Dae-jung on March 20, 2002, for Commerce and Industry Day, where he praised our company's export contributions and invited me to play a significant role in the upcoming World Cup.

The Special Achievement Award I received in 2008 for the 60th Anniversary of the National Foundation was particularly special, as it was bestowed upon only four business leaders recognized for their substantial contributions to exports and for setting an exemplary standard. In the same year, Ilsung recorded exports of $180 million and was also awarded the $100 million export tower.

The 2009 Trader of the Year Award Who Glorified Korea, which I received, filled me with pride. It was awarded to the CEO with the most outstanding export activities among the 64,000 member companies of the trade association in 2009.

I also want to note that 2010 became an unforgettable year for me. It was not only the year when Ilsung achieved $200 million in exports, but also personally significant as I received the Gold Tower Order of Industrial Service Merit on November 30th, the 47th

Trade Day. This award is the highest honor for an exporter.

Reflecting on these honorable accolades, I realized that these were not solely the result of my efforts, but rather the culmination of the hard work and dedication of all Ilsung employees, as well as the support of our society and nation. I am indebted to the Ilsung team, our community, and the country. My responsibility now is to reciprocate their kindness.

While I established Ilsung to create my own path, its development has reached a point where it is no longer mine alone. Just as a country belongs to its people, Ilsung now belongs to its employees, not just to me. Ilsung Industry, once a private company, has evolved into a leading export company, transcending the boundaries of a private enterprise to become a social entity. Throughout its history, I have fostered trusting relationships with employees and business partners based on this philosophy, enjoying the glory that came with Ilsung's development. Now, my remaining task is to share the blessings I've received with those who have been gracious to me. The rest of my life is dedicated to fulfilling this purpose.

THE LOCALIZATION OF PETROCHEMICAL PLANTS IS THE KEY!

Until the mid-1990s, when Ilsung began to export in earnest, over 90% of its sales were from the domestic market. However, once the focus shifted to overseas markets, the domestic sales dropped to only 10%, with exports accounting for 90%. This shift marked Ilsung's emergence as a fully-fledged export company. A key factor behind Ilsung's rise as a leading export company in Korea is the localization of technology.

In fact, the drive to localize technology for petrochemical plants was one of the main reasons I founded Ilsung. During my tenure at an oil company, I was disheartened by the reliance on imported parts. I believed that with additional research and effort, these components could be produced domestically, yet this idea seemed to draw no interest within the company. As I honed my skills, my confidence in the potential of domestic production of these parts and equipment grew. After establishing Ilsung, my primary business goal was to develop local production technology for petrochemical plants.

Initially, I faced the challenge of having to import every component, even the smallest parts. The process involved importing individual parts and then welding and connecting them to assemble equipment, which was far from straightforward. Additionally, the high unit prices necessitated setting low margins. Therefore, the localization of technology for building petrochemical plants became the most significant challenge I had to confront.

Equipment and parts for petrochemical plants require specialized technology to withstand high temperatures and pressures. At that time, most people were unfamiliar with even the basic production processes. However, drawing on my experience at an oil company, I embraced the challenge of developing and producing these components domestically. While people often travel to advanced countries to learn technology, I chose a different path. A critical aspect of manufacturing and selling parts is meeting and passing inspection regulations. I focused particularly on these regulations, understanding that passing them signified a technological achievement. My efforts were concentrated on creating parts that met inspection standards, especially those of American regulations. Gradually, we started achieving domestic production of petrochemical plant parts, one by one. Eventually, Ilsung succeeded in constructing a petrochemical plant using 100% domestic technology, a first in Korea. This 100%

achievement did not occur overnight; it was a gradual process over 10 years. Yet, from my perspective, it seemed to happen suddenly. This was because I was not aiming to achieve local production by a specific deadline, but rather focused on the local production of each part sequentially. Consequently, when Ilsung finally produced the last remaining part domestically, it felt as though everything had come together suddenly, all at once.

The successful construction of a petrochemical plant by Ilsung, utilizing 100% domestic technology, signified more than mere domestic production. It demonstrated that our domestic technology had attained an international standard, aligning Ilsung's petrochemical plant technology with global levels.

Achieving full localization in petrochemical plant construction held additional significance for Ilsung. For the company, it opened the door to higher profits, as it allowed for greater margins than when importing all parts and equipment. This achievement also enhanced Ilsung's reputation for technological expertise and product quality. As a result, Ilsung began receiving orders from leading global companies, facilitating its transition from a domestically focused enterprise to an export-oriented one.

Moreover, Ilsung's accomplishment in fully localizing its technology holds social importance. It bolstered the company's reputation within the local community and naturally enhanced its corporate image. Consequently, Ilsung earned several awards and emerged as a nationally recognized export company.

People often inquire about the secret behind Ilsung's success in achieving 100% domestication of technology. Sometimes, I find this question challenging to answer, simply because there isn't a specific secret to our success. However, if I were to identify a key factor, it would be my management philosophy, which placed utmost importance on technology and emphasized continuous technical training for our employees. During that period, I personally bought technical books and distributed them among employees to encourage skill development. Additionally, the company dedicated itself to technical education, initiating a 'campaign for national technical certification for technicians' that involved all 350 employees. These efforts led to Ilsung being recognized as an 'Excellent Skills Encouragement Company' by the Ministry of Labor three times consecutively – in 1992, 1996, and 2001. The 'technical certification campaign', sustained over a decade, became a deep-rooted tradition, instilling pride and a sense of accomplishment in Ilsung employees. To directly address the question of our secret, I would point to these concerted efforts as the key.

Now, I would like to outline Ilsung's technological milestones by year, from its inception until it reached $200 million in exports in 2010.

Apr. 1984	Obtained license for facility and steel structure construction, electrical work and thermal equipment manufacturing
Sept. 1986	Registered as a gas facility public business operator and obtained import & export permit
Mar. 1989	Acquired high-pressure gas specific equipment manufacturing license
Nov. 1989	Earned ASME stamps in 3 categories
Oct. 1992	Designated as an excellent technology-aware company by the Korean government
Oct. 1994	Obtained ISO 9001 certification issued by TUV
Jul. 1994	Received the Production Improvement Excellence Award from the Korean government
Nov. 1995	Received the prestigious New Korea Award in the field of new technology
Oct. 1996	Designated as an excellent technology-aware company by the Korean government
Dec. 1998	Receives new "U2" ASME stamp
Nov. 2004	Acquired ISO 14001 certification from Korea Gas Safety Corporation
Jul. 2005	Registered as an approved supplier with SABIC
Apr. 2006	Acquired Saudi Aramco's Quality Management System (QMS) approval

Dec. 2006	Obtained OHSAS 18001 certification from Korea Gas Safety Corporation
Aug. 2007	Acquired Helix Exchanger license from Lummus Technology Inc.
Apr. 2009	Acquired 'Breech-Lock Exchanger' license from Lummus Technology Inc.
Aug. 2009	Acquired KEPIC-MN & KEPIC-SN certificate issued by Korea Electric Association
Dec. 2010	Obtained "U2" ASME stamp

CHAPTER 2

SMALL DETAILS, THE DRIVE BEHIND GROWTH

A WHOLE IS NOTHING BUT THE SUM OF SMALL PARTS

THE REASON ILSUNG DREW THE ATTENTION OF THE WORLD
COMPETENCY AND TRUST EARNED THROUGH ATTENTION TO LITTLE DETAILS

Since its inception, Ilsung has consistently produced results and continued to develop, despite facing several challenges and crises, which I will detail separately later. The company was also recognized for its technological prowess by global companies, rising to the status of a leading export company. In Buddhism, there's a concept known as the law of cause and effect, positing that every outcome is the result of a cause. Reflecting on this principle, one might wonder what led to Ilsung's remarkable achievements. How did a small business like Ilsung gain recognition from global companies? Looking back, I find our accomplishments astonishing and a source of pride. In my approach to work, I don't rely on learned secrets; instead, I work based on experience and intuition. That's why I often struggle to respond when asked about the 'secret' to our success. The difficulty in pinpointing the secret of Ilsung's success lies in the fact that I've always relied on my experience and intuition, quietly performing the task at hand. Everything unfolded as a result of this approach.

In the midst of my commitment to business, I seldom had the opportunity to logically ponder the 'secret' behind my success. However, now, as I reflect on my life and undertake the task of writing a book, I feel compelled to delve deeply into this matter. As I mentioned at the beginning of this book, my aim is not merely to chronicle my life but also to instill dreams, hopes, and a spirit of challenge in the younger generation.

Today, we live in what can be described as an era of hardship, so pervasive that many consider it a natural consequence of a competitive society. However, I believe that the older generations shirk their responsibility if they fail to offer guidance and alternatives to the youth. My intention is to use my 60 years of experience and knowledge to infuse the younger generation with a spirit of challenge, dreams, hopes, and skills. In this context, identifying a logical explanation for the results achieved by myself and Ilsung became an important task. This introspection led me to scrutinize every detail of my life, allowing me to discern a logical cause for my achievements.

I am aware that the market is flooded with books offering numerous secrets to achieving results and succeeding in one's career. As an avid reader who draws a great deal of information and strength from books, I am quite familiar with the 'secrets' these books discuss. While some readers may find these self-help books tremendously beneficial, I have often felt that, although there are aspects I reso-

nate with, other parts seem lacking. Therefore, in my book, I aim to present my insights in a way that does not merely reiterate the stereotypical content found in existing literature.

To be straightforward, I believe that 'skill' and a 'trust relationship' are crucial to achieving results in any endeavor. Let's consider how I founded Ilsung and secured my first order. My first order was maintenance work for the oil company where I had worked before. The company entrusted me with this job because they recognized my skills and also because I had a trusting relationship with them.

For achievements like this, competency and trust are indispensable. For instance, consider Ilsung's long-term preferred supplier agreement (EFA: Enterprise Frame Agreement) with the global company Shell. I take pride in the fact that Ilsung was chosen as the sole Ko-

Opposition party leader Kim Jong-pil's visit to the company

rean partner, as it reflects our esteemed status. It raises the question: How could a global company like Shell enter into such a contract with Ilsung, a medium-sized Korean company? This was made possible because Shell recognized Ilsung's technological capabilities and a trust relationship had been established between the two. If Ilsung's technical skills had been even slightly subpar, Shell would not have signed a contract with us. Similarly, no matter the extent of Ilsung's proven capabilities, Shell would not have considered a contract if a trustful relationship was not in place. Hence, both capabilities and trust are crucial, to the extent that lacking either one would impede successful collaboration.

Later, when Ilsung faced bankruptcy and entered court receivership, it seemed inevitable that the EFA supply contract would be terminated. On a rainy Friday afternoon, my eldest son, in charge of management, received a call from Shell. Expecting the worst, he answered, bracing for news about the contract's termination. Surprisingly, Shell began by expressing empathy and condolences for Ilsung's court receivership. Confused, my son anticipated the next words to be about breaking the contract. However, as the conversation continued, Shell conveyed trust in our past performance and belief in our efforts during these difficult times. Despite the bankruptcy and court receivership, Shell affirmed its commitment to maintaining its partnership with us.

In response, my son, filled with gratitude and tears on that rainy Friday afternoon in March, expressed his heartfelt thanks to Shell. He vowed never to forget Shell's support during such a challenging time. It was both unforgettable and unexpected. As a result, our relationship with Shell remains strong, and we are proud to continue as Korea's sole supplier to Shell.

It's important to recognize that capabilities and trust have different levels: high, medium, and low. When both capabilities and trust are at a high level, peak performance is achieved. Conversely, if both are at a low level, the performance is likely to be poor. To attain a higher level of performance, it's crucial to enhance both capabilities and trust. This is a key principle. Pursuing excellence in capabilities and nurturing trusting relationships has enabled Ilsung to emerge as a leading export company, conducting business with top companies worldwide. This, you could say, is the secret behind Ilsung's success.

So, the question arises: How does one build top-level capabilities and a trusting relationship? I will delve into this topic in the forthcoming sections of this book. The essence of my message revolves around this very point. I will frequently use the term 'small details,' and I encourage readers to pay close attention to this concept as you progress through the book.

SaDe is an abbreviation for 'small details,' a term I've coined to emphasize the significance of paying attention to the minutest details that are often overlooked.

SADE MAKES A BIG DIFFERENCE IN SKILLS

I recall a televised debate battle, reminiscent of a boxing match in a ring, where participants engaged in a debate until a winner was declared. Unlike typical debates characterized by argumentative exchanges, this one captivated the audience, who watched with bated breath as two individuals fiercely debated. To maintain the debaters' anonymity, I'll refer to them as A and B. A was renowned as 'the king of debate,' so naturally, people expected A to triumph. However, as the debate progressed, an unexpected turn of events unfolded: A was outmaneuvered, and B, gaining momentum, won in less than an hour. Why did this happen?

Many were puzzled by A's defeat, given his superior debating skills, but I quickly discerned the cause. It was the gap created by a difference in attention to details. Although A was technically more skilled, he lacked thorough preparation on the debate topic compared to B, leading to his decisive defeat.

To better illustrate the kind of details I'm referring to, let's consider the debate topic was 'the relationship between foreign exchange reserves and foreign exchange crises.' Economic issues are inherently complex, and even among economists, definitive answers are rare. However, in a debate where not all participants are economic experts, the outcome often hinges on who prepares more meticulously.

Let's imagine that the debaters in this scenario are C and D, with C being the more competitive debater of the two. C, somewhat underestimating D, entered the debate armed only with the basic knowledge that the size of foreign exchange reserves influences foreign exchange crises. However, D, with determination, prepared for the debate by studying more than ten related papers.

C argued that a foreign exchange crisis occurred in the past when foreign exchange reserves were critically low, necessitating IMF involvement. He reasoned that, given the current sizeable foreign exchange reserves, a similar crisis would not occur. D, however, countered this argument by stating that a foreign exchange crisis cannot be judged solely by the size of the reserves. He emphasized that a crisis assessment requires a detailed examination of the reserves to determine the actual available amount during a crisis. D then detailed Korea's current foreign exchange reserves situation: a total of $430 billion, with only 6.9% in reserves and the remaining 93.1% in bonds, securities, and stocks. He pointed out that, in a crisis, only 6.9% of these reserves would be readily available.

Further elucidating his point, D compared this with Korea's reserves during the 2008 financial crisis. At that time, Korea had $200 billion in reserves, with 8% in deposits and 92% in bonds, securities, and stocks. He explained that, while the $200 billion at that time was roughly equivalent to the current $430 billion, the actual liquid funds available were only 8% of the total. D concluded by explaining that this was why the Korean economy was severely impacted during the foreign exchange crisis.

However, D further argued that since the actual accessible funds now constitute only 6.9% of the total reserves, which is even lower than during the 2008 financial crisis, the Korean economy could be more vulnerable in the event of a new crisis. His rationale was that, given this reduced percentage of readily available funds, the Korean economy might collapse if faced with another foreign exchange crisis, unable to fend it off effectively. With such a marked difference in attention to details, it's not hard to foresee who would emerge victorious in the debate.

Now, with this example in mind, can you grasp the significance of the impact that SaDe, or attention to 'small details,' can have?

The difference in SaDe immediately leads to a difference in level. Earlier, I mentioned that if you want to achieve greater success, you should raise your skills to a higher level. However, it's important to note that advanced skills are developed precisely by focusing on small details. In other words, the more you concentrate on SaDe, the more your skills will improve.

The difference in SaDe immediately leads to a difference in level. Earlier, I mentioned that if you want to achieve greater success, you should raise your skills to a higher level. However, it's important to note that advanced skills are developed precisely by focusing on small details. In other words, the more you concentrate on SaDe, the more your skills will improve.

Many people wonder about the secret behind Ilsung's global recognition. I believe it's largely due to our meticulous attention to small details. Ilsung's commitment to SaDe involved not only skill development, as mentioned earlier, but also fostering a trusting relationship. This focus enabled Ilsung to first gain recognition in the domestic market and subsequently in the global arena. Moving forward, let's explore how SaDe influences skill development and trust, elevating them to the highest level.

SADE BEGINS WITH UNDERSTANDING THE SIGNIFICANCE OF EVEN THE SMALLEST COMPONENTS WITHIN THE WHOLE!

It's possible that some readers are still unclear about the concept of SaDe as I've described it. To simplify, SaDe can be defined as 'the ability to accurately identify problems without overlooking any details, no matter how small or seemingly insignificant.' People often pay attention to what they deem important, yet frequently disregard what they consider trivial, failing to give those aspects the attention they deserve.

However, there's remarkable value hidden in these little details. People feel appreciated when you remember and celebrate what's important to them, like their birthdays. But they are truly delighted when you acknowledge and act upon the things that are more trivial than their birthdays. This observation highlights the extraordinary significance of seemingly minor details. This concept is also echoed in the book *Money-making Habits*, where the author discusses how slight differences in habits can determine whether people become rich or poor. It's the small things, such as the way one thinks, speaks, and acts, that differentiate the wealthy from the poor. Wealthy individuals think, speak, and act in ways characteristic of their status, while those less affluent often overlook the importance of these aspects, adhering to their usual habits. Even with the various efforts to amass wealth, unless they focus more on these small details, they are unlikely to become rich, regardless of their attempts to build wealth. In this manner, trivialities wield immense power, shaping who becomes wealthy and who does not.

One aspect often overlooked is the importance of everyday elements like sunlight and air. We tend to take these for granted because they're always present. But imagine a world without sunlight and air; human survival would be impossible. This exemplifies the profound impact of seemingly insignificant things. Despite their importance, these elements are often ignored because of their constant presence. While birthdays, occurring once a year, are acknowledged for their significance, daily routines, due to their repetitive nature, tend to be overlooked. Yet, it's crucial to understand that attention to these routine aspects is essential for a fulfilling life.

The principle of SaDe is equally relevant in the workplace. Consider a successful restaurant, where the owner meticulously oversees every detail, from parking services to the dining hall to the kitchen. In contrast, a failing restaurant often lacks attention to these small details, leading to visible problems. This highlights that success is often achieved by those who focus on even the minutest aspects of their work.

My understanding of the law of SaDe deepened through fieldwork experiences. For instance, observing welders, I noticed that they often don't see a mistake until something goes wrong. This process of correcting and re-inspecting is time-consuming and inefficient. This inefficiency stems from a lack of attention to detail at the outset. Had they focused more on details before starting their welding work, much time and cost could have been saved. This is a clear example of the consequences when details are neglected.

Many perceive welding as a simple manual task, yet the intricacies involved in welding—from posture, skills, and purpose to the type of welding—are not as straightforward as one might think. If a welding job is approached with a comprehensive understanding of these details, many errors and unnecessary costs can be significantly reduced. However, common issues arise when ordinary welders overlook these minor details. Broadening this perspective, it becomes apparent that such problems often fall under the responsibility of field supervisors. The time and cost inefficiencies encountered are usually due to the supervisors' failure to attend to the smallest details.

I came to this realization early in my fieldwork, leading to my discovery of the law of SaDe. By implementing this principle at Ilsung, I was instrumental in transforming the company into a globally recognized entity.

SADE IS EVERYTHING
A WHOLE IS THE SUM OF ITS SMALLEST DETAILS

Some might argue that an excessive focus on minor details could lead to losing sight of the bigger picture. This is akin to the well-known analogy of trees and a forest: focusing solely on the trees means you miss the forest, and vice versa. This metaphor is central to understanding SaDe. The aim of SaDe is to meticulously study each detail of a tree, ensuring no minor aspect is overlooked, in order to fully comprehend the entire forest.

It's crucial to realize that the SaDe I am discussing begins with an overview. Analogous to the forest and trees story, it involves first observing the forest and then examining the individual trees to gain a comprehensive understanding of the forest. In essence, we must remember that the purpose of paying attention to minor details is as a means to thoroughly understand the whole.

SaDe is a tool for gaining a deeper and broader understanding of the bigger picture. The more we know about even the smallest details within the context of the whole, the more profoundly and expansively we can comprehend the entirety. This understanding forms the essence of the SaDe concept.

When I was first tasked with supervising fieldwork, I pondered deeply on how to effectively manage the overall assignments. Typically, many supervisors adhere to traditional customs and methods, leaving little room for innovation. I was determined not to simply follow in others' footsteps. This led me to develop SaDe as my unique approach. By applying SaDe to the entire work process, I found that it resulted in a more effective whole.

In this light, I believe SaDe is paramount. Essentially, SaDe and the whole are one and the same. The whole is comprised of details, much like a puzzle is made of interlocking pieces. Consider a ballpoint pen as an example. When viewed as a whole, it consists of various components: the ball enabling ink to transfer to paper, the surrounding tip, the ink cartridge and spring, and the body housing these parts. Who would have a better understanding of the ballpoint pen? Someone who only observes its external appearance, or someone who is familiar with all these internal components? Delving even deeper, understanding the materials that make up the pen's ink and ball leads to an even more comprehensive understanding than someone who only knows its components.

Now, can you grasp the connection between details and the bigger picture? The SaDe I champion is a method to gain a deeper understanding of the whole. The more intricately you comprehend even the tiniest details within the framework of the whole, the more profound and expansive your understanding of the entire system becomes. This understanding is at the heart of the SaDe concept. In this sense, it can be said that SaDe encapsulates the formula, "Whole = SaDe × SaDe".

Whole = SaDe × SaDe

In applying the SaDe concept, I emphasize a multiplication approach over addition. This is because, in the realm of SaDe, the whole operates on a multiplicative dimension rather than an additive one. While addition can produce synergy, it falls short of achieving the utmost potential. Multiplication, on the other hand, is instrumental in elevating skills to a higher level. For instance, 10+10 equals 20, but 10×10 equals 100. The number 100 represents a transformative leap to a different level. By immersing oneself in SaDe within the broader context, you may eventually find that your skills have significantly advanced. Reaching this point means your abilities are maximized, creating a substantial gap between you and others. In this light, SaDe emerges as the optimal method to maximize one's skills.

TECHNICAL ACHIEVEMENTS AND SKILLS ACHIEVED THROUGH SADE

For a field supervisor, completing work assignments flawlessly within the set deadline is paramount. In construction, time equates to money, so finishing work earlier than the promised date equates to saving both time and cost, representing the best possible outcome in the field.

Even with the same job, some companies may take 15 days, while others may finish in just a week, yet the quality of the work remains comparable. From a business standpoint, which company would you trust and value more? Logically, management would naturally favor the on-site supervisor who completed the work in a week. During my tenure at an oil company, I became curious about the source of this discrepancy. After observing for a week, I discovered that the supervisor who finished in a week had prepared more meticulously in advance. Delving deeper into their performance, I noticed that this supervisor paid attention to even the smallest details and planned thoroughly before commencing work. In contrast, the supervisor who took 15 days overlooked minor details and neglected them, failing to address them proactively. This realization was like a Eureka moment for me, marking the beginning of my study into SaDe.

While working for the oil company, most of my work assignments involved fieldwork. Therefore, after I established Ilsung, I immediately started implementing the law of SaDe in my work. In the specialized field of technology, it's common to encounter obstacles when delving into details. It's crucial not to give up during these times. With the right mindset, you can decipher the correct techniques for most technologies. Some technologies, however, are more complex. Even in these cases, you can usually find a solution by seeking additional study materials or consulting a technology research institute for extra help.

I applied the law of SaDe to virtually every aspect of my work, from technology development to product creation in the field. This approach enabled Ilsung to consistently deliver or complete orders well ahead of schedule, saving both time and costs, and boosting company profits.

A significant achievement for Ilsung was the 100% localization of technology for plant equipment, accomplished solely through the law of SaDe. While others sought to learn technology from advanced countries, I managed to achieve complete localization of production using this law. The technology developed by Ilsung was not only on par with that of advanced countries but was often considered more advanced.

One of the secrets behind Ilsung's rise as an industry leader, recognized globally, is its world-class technology. As previously mentioned, Ilsung has acquired numerous technical qualifications and technology patents. These technological achievements led to the company receiving the Production Improvement Excellence Award from the Korean government, as well as the prestigious New Korea Award in the new technology field. Additionally, the Korean government has recognized the company as an excellent technology-aware entity. All these achievements stem from successfully applying the law of SaDe in the technological domain. This underlines the significance of the law of SaDe, which focuses on attention to the smallest details.

The law of SaDe emphasizes the importance of paying attention to details and not overlooking minor aspects, and that is a key factor in skill development. Essentially, the disparity in skills is reflected in the application of SaDe. Individuals with lower skills possess knowledge and experience that has not delved into detail, whereas those with higher skills have detailed knowledge and experience. To enhance your skills, remember this principle and focus on studying even the smallest details.

SADE ALSO APPLIES TO TRUSTING RELATIONSHIPS!

Let's reflect on the time when Ilsung was exploring the Iranian market. I initially sent our employees for negotiations. After their return, they reported having done everything possible and were simply awaiting a call. However, when no call came, I sensed something was amiss. Inquiring further, the employees confirmed they had submitted the quotation as planned, but were equally puzzled by the lack of response. At that moment, I realized there was a disparity between the perspectives of the employees and myself, the owner. While I was extremely anxious, the employees appeared nonchalant, content with passively waiting for a response rather than actively seeking one.

I subsequently retrained my employees on appropriate actions in such situations. I emphasized the importance of viewing the scenario from the potential client's perspective. Consider the choice between a company that submits a quote and waits, versus one that establishes rapport through regular follow-ups, inquiries about missing elements, or offers advice. Naturally, the more proactive company tends to garner more interest. A passive approach, limited to just providing a quote, often leads to missed opportunities, which go unrecognized due to a lack of close communication with the prospective client. This becomes evident when, upon belated contact, the company is informed that another, more engaged company was chosen, often citing a slightly higher quote. This underlines the importance of proactive communication in building trusting business relationships.

The reason I meticulously attend to even the smallest details is to keep my promises to customers accurately. This practice is vital for receiving orders and sustaining the company.

The law of SaDe, which I apply to such details, extends to human relationships as well. Sales are largely about human connections, and success in sales hinges on turning these into trusting relationships. The same law of SaDe that I've utilized in technology is equally applicable to human interactions. It involves focusing on the minutiae within. As I mentioned earlier, They are happy when you remember and celebrate their birthdays, but they are even more delighted when you acknowledge and commemorate the lesser occasions and it can significantly enhance a relationship, embodying the essence of the law of SaDe in human connections.

This attention to detail is as important in human relationships as it is in technology development. For example, when visiting a customer, I strive to empathize and act from their perspective. A case in point: I once traveled to London, England, and took an expensive taxi to a remote location to meet engineers from a Saudi company. This effort demonstrated my commitment to detail. Moreover, discovering and catering to a person's interests to foster familiarity is part of this detailed approach. Merely establishing a business relationship is superficial and lacks depth. When a customer visits, offering thoughtful services, such as ensuring a comfortable journey from the airport to your company, may seem minor but can significantly impact and foster trust with the customer.

Having applied the law of SaDe to human relationships for a long time, I've honed the ability to understand people through their eyes, facial expressions, and posture. I can often determine at first meeting whether someone will be a suitable fit or if I should avoid engaging with them. This skill, such as discerning an issue from an engineer's facial expression during my trip to pioneer the Iranian market, is a product of my extensive experience in human interactions. It's important to recognize that this perceptive ability is a part of the law of SaDe as it applies to human relationships.

When the law of SaDe is applied to human interaction, it cultivates trusting relationships. The principle of forming trust through SaDe in human interactions parallels its application in technology. Just as applying SaDe in technology leads to advanced capabilities and earns customers' trust in the technology, applying it to human interactions enhances the quality of those interactions, fostering natural trust.

Crucial in this process is the attitude with which you apply the law of SaDe to human relationships. As the practitioner, you must approach others with trust, since the ultimate goal is to establish a trusting relationship. Trusting the other person first is imperative for them to trust you in return. If you approach someone with suspicion, how can you expect them to trust you? This mutual trust is at the core of applying the law of SaDe effectively in human relationships.

Ilsung is renowned for its non-union management. However, it's not that I have been against union formation; rather, our employees haven't felt the need to form a union due to the trust established between me, as the owner, and them. This trusting relationship is the result of my deliberate efforts to apply the law of SaDe in human interactions. The specifics of Ilsung's non-union management will be addressed separately.

THE LAW OF SADE APPLIES TO ALL FIELDS

I have discussed how the law of SaDe is crucial in developing trust and skills. But upon closer examination, you'll find that this law can be applied to all facets of life. The law of SaDe is not limited to the economy; it extends to politics, society, family life, and even the personal growth of individuals. This is because the law of SaDe aims to elevate not only the economy but also political, social, familial, and individual realms. Consider this: if the standards in our country's politics, economy, society, family, and individual lives improve, wouldn't the Republic of Korea not only ascend to the ranks of truly advanced countries but also enhance the quality of life for its citizens?

THE LAW OF SADE APPLIED IN POLITICAL COMMUNICATION

Many people express concern that Korea's politics is regressing. I'll delve into this more later, but it's important to note that Ilsung faced significant challenges due to the KIKO (Knock-In, Knock-Out) incident, which involved derivative contracts on foreign exchange rates and had connections to the political community. The KIKO (Knock-In, Knock-Out) incident escalated into a national economic problem after affecting hundreds of small and medium-sized businesses, which suffered significant losses. I had meetings with government officials and political leaders to resolve this issue. It later became known that this incident was connected to the political community. As a Christian, I pray for my country, but sometimes these prayers leave me feeling heartbroken. It's disheartening to witness politics entrenched in left-right divisions, consumed with criticism and conflict, yet lacking a genuine focus on the populace's welfare and the nation's development.

Politics in our country is often perceived as a field for those who have reached a certain level of success in various societal sectors. But why is it so backward? I believe this backwardness stems from a neglect of details in politics.

By applying the law of SaDe to political communication, we can address these issues. Political communication should encompass dialogue between the president and the citizens. Unfortunately, in our country, this communication is not effectively executed. I consider this poor communication a primary reason for the backwardness in our country's politics.

Why is political communication not happening? Could it be due to a lack of communication experts in political groups, where the most talented individuals from various fields gather? I believe these groups do have communication experts. However, communication remains ineffective because it is often dismissed as trivial in politics. In our country, the primary focus of politics appears to be on gaining power, leading to ongoing competition between the ruling and opposition parties. The secondary priority seems to be formulating policies that appeal to the public, though this too is ultimately aimed at gaining power, with both sides competing over policies as well.

In such a political culture, where does communication stand? It likely ranks low on the list of priorities. Consequently, detailed communication skills are underdeveloped, explaining the lack of effective communication in politics. Developing even minor communication skills requires extensive study and effort. For instance, the Moon Jae-in administration created the 'National Sinmungo' system for its style of communication, but its transformation into a platform for political conflict highlights the administration's limited communication skills.

The solution lies in recognizing the importance of communication, even if it seems trivial, and applying the law of SaDe in political contexts. When the level of communication improves and the political community begins to engage effectively with the public, it will, in turn, elevate the overall standard of politics.

THE LAW OF SADE APPLIED TO FAMILY COMMUNICATION

The Law of SaDe is also relevant in our homes. Today, we see a growing number of families in crisis, alongside an increasing reluctance to marry. This trend, I believe, stems from a societal shift: society is evolving, yet our family dynamics remain unchanged. Families, as the fundamental unit of social organization, provide a nurturing environment where individuals care for each other and raise future generations. The strength and stability of a society, and by extension the nation, are deeply rooted in the health of its family units. Thus, the disintegration of family structures is not just a personal issue but a warning sign for societal and national wellbeing. Consequently, enhancing family values and fostering peaceful family environments should be a paramount objective in our society.

How, then, can we elevate the standards of our homes? One effective method is by applying the Law of SaDe, with a focus on enhancing family communication. Healthy family dynamics hinge on open and regular interactions among family members. When communication is obstructed, it can lead to familial discord, similar to how blocked arteries can damage the heart. Unfortunately,

Understanding our thoughts and emotions through a detailed study of our inner selves not only initiates a process of correction but also lays the groundwork for personal growth. This transformation of the inner self is crucial in an era that demands deep self-development.

even in domestic settings, communication is often overlooked and deemed unimportant compared to material achievements. For instance, many families in Korea prioritize financial success, housing upgrades, and educational opportunities for children over nurturing family ties.

However, if communication were recognized as a fundamental aspect of family life, we could significantly reduce familial breakdowns. Whether in a family, society, or nation, the root of many issues lies in a lack of effective communication. Hence, prioritizing dialogue over material gains and developing detailed communication strategies within families is essential. By cultivating a culture that values communication, the prevalence of disjointed family units could be drastically reduced worldwide.

INNER GROWTH THROUGH THE LAW OF SADE

The Law of SaDe's true brilliance, I believe, lies in its applicability to inner growth. Observing the inner lives of people in society today, it seems they are as fragile as a thin glass window braving a typhoon. If we consider our societal challenges as a typhoon, then the inner world of modern individuals appears perilously fragile. Can such a delicate barrier withstand such a storm? This metaphor reflects the instability faced by many today, leading to widespread issues like depression and panic disorder. Moreover, this fragility can sometimes culminate in tragic decisions. For instance, Korea's high suicide rate is a stark indicator of the need for greater inner resilience. Why do these outcomes occur? In my view, this can be attributed to a matter of inner maturity. These results arise because our inner selves mature slower than society processes.

INNER MATURITY THROUGH THE LAW OF SADE

So, how can we achieve maturity of our inner self? Applying the law of SaDe to elevate our inner selves is a promising approach. By delving into the human inner world, we recognize its composition of thoughts, emotions, and feelings. Our emotions are influenced by our thoughts, emphasizing the importance of both. Therefore, the quality of our inner life hinges on the nature of our thoughts and emotions. Cultivating a healthy mental and emotional state is key to developing a strong, resilient inner self, capable of withstanding life's challenges.

What Controls Our Thoughts and Emotions? Our thoughts and emotions are largely influenced by the values and worldview we develop through life experiences and accumulated knowledge. When confronted with a situation or problem, our reactions — in the form of feelings and emotions — are shaped by these internal frameworks. If our values and worldview are skewed towards negativity, this predisposition can manifest itself in negative thoughts and speech. Over time, these can solidify into habits, shaping us into individuals who predominantly think and speak negatively.

Moreover, our emotions are directed by our thoughts. Predominantly negative thoughts foster negative emotions such as anger, worry, and anxiety. These emotions can have a destructive impact on our well-being. This process illustrates the mechanism by which our inner self operates.

By understanding and analyzing these inner workings, we can initiate a process of correction. Recognizing and adjusting our values and worldview can transform our inner self, laying a strong foundation for personal growth and positive change.

I often feel saddened when I see people easily giving up in the face of difficult challenges. I firmly believe that any problem, no matter how daunting, can be overcome. This belief was even reinforced during my own challenging experience with the KIKO incident, which I will elaborate on later. When I was imprisoned due to this incident, I chose to use the time for self-reflection and personal growth, rather than succumbing to anger or despair. An ancient proverb states that one can survive even in a tiger's den as long as one remains alert. However, this resilience is a testament to inner strength, something that seems scarce in today's society. There is an urgent need for us to introspect, to delve into the details of our inner selves, and to cultivate our inner strength.

CHAPTER 3

THE ORIGIN OF MY BELIEF IN SADE

MY EXTRAORDINARY INTUITION EXPERIENCE

CHILDHOOD SPENT IN JAPAN

All humans have a past, present, and future in their lives. These temporal states are not separate entities; they are organically interconnected, much like living organisms. My past has shaped who I am today, and my actions today will determine who I become tomorrow. In this regard, reflecting on my past is crucial to understanding my current self. Such reflection helps in comprehending how the principles of attention to detail, trust, and belief that I advocate have developed over time.

Discussing my birthplace brings a sense of embarrassment, as I have concealed the fact that I was born in Japan for many years. During my travels abroad, I always introduced myself as being born in Korea, not Japan. Reflecting on this, I realize that it was likely driven by my pride for Korea. Therefore, revealing the truth about my birthplace holds significant meaning for me now.

I was born in 1939, the eldest of six children, in Beppu, a city in the former Mamoto prefecture of Kyushu, Japan's southernmost island. Beppu is renowned for its hot springs. While hot springs are common throughout Japan, Beppu is celebrated for having the largest number of vents. As far as I remember, my parents were in Japan at the time of my birth because my father had moved there to work in a coal mine.

I recall that there were almost no Koreans in the neighborhood where I was born, and I vividly remember playing with Japanese kids around the area. My next-door neighbor had a child about my age, and we often played together. However, one day we had a fight, and I hit him. I don't remember exactly what led to the altercation. The Japanese boy cried, and his father went searching for the child who had hit his son. He accused a Korean elementary student from our neighborhood, mistakenly blaming him for something I had done. Perhaps he never suspected me, being only about four years old at the time. Consequently, the elementary student was wrongfully accused of hitting the Japanese boy.

After that incident, our family moved from Beppu to a rural village. My father explained that the move was necessary due to the difficulty of making a living in Beppu. Life in the village was mostly peaceful. Our house was surrounded by rice fields and enclosed with a bamboo fence. It was during the late stages of the Pacific War, and whenever U.S. military planes launched air raids, we had to hide in a bunker, resembling an underground cave, for days on end. My father worked as a farmer in this village. I spent my days swimming and playing in a large stream, about 50 meters wide, located a few hundred meters from our village. One day, while swimming, I injured myself on something along the riverbank and started bleeding. There was no one around to help, so I remember making my way back home, attempting to stop the bleeding on my own, despite being just a four-year-old boy.

ON THE WAY BACK TO THE HOMELAND AFTER LIBERATION

In the meantime, Korea had been liberated from Japanese rule. My father, eager to return to our homeland, hurried to make arrangements for our departure. At that time, Koreans returning home from Japan typically traveled via ship from Shimonoseki Port. Fortunately, my family managed to secure passage on a ship crossing the treacherous Tsushima Strait. However, the journey was not smooth; due to strong waves, our ship had to anchor at Tsushima Island. With uncertainty looming over when we might depart again, all passengers, including my family, disembarked with their luggage.

While waiting on the island, we heard troubling news. One of the two anchored ships had been set adrift by strong winds and had disappeared. This incident caused fear and concern among the people, worried they might not be able to return to their homeland if conditions didn't improve. Even as a young boy, I vividly recall

Now in my 80s, I remember in sharp detail the times in my youth when I overcame fears and achieved success. These moments have become the foundation and a significant driving force in my journey from humble beginnings to where I am now. This particular experience remains etched in my heart as a pivotal detail in my growth and has continually inspired me to expand my company and surmount challenges.

hearing this story and feeling a sudden surge of fear.

Fortunately, the wind had subsided, allowing the boat to stabilize. My family prepared to reboard the ship with our luggage. As the eldest child, with a newborn sister in tow, the responsibility was significant. My mother, carrying her on her back, and my father, laden with our bags, instructed me to board the ship first. Despite the calmer wind, the waves were still strong, causing the ship, a weather-beaten ferry, to rock intensely. Approaching the stairs to the ship, the sight of the turbulent blue sea crashing against them filled me with dread. I realized that one misstep could be fatal. In that moment, feeling isolated and overwhelmed, tears began to well up in my eyes. I knew I had to muster the courage to ascend the stairs and ensure my survival. Drawing on all my strength, I managed to climb aboard. The thrill that I felt at that moment still resonates with me to this day.

I was aboard the ship, which had resumed its journey, when I suddenly felt the need to use the bathroom. As a six-year-old, my search for a restroom led me to a daunting discovery: the only facility available was a large hole in the deck. To me, this hole appeared immense and menacing. Peering down, I saw the blue waves swelling beneath, seemingly ready to engulf me. The urgent need to relieve myself was at odds with my fear of this intimidating hole.

In the end, I made a choice. Trembling with fear, I stood over the gaping opening that served as the ship's toilet, staring into the churning blue abyss below. The thought of falling in was terrifying;

it felt like flirting with death. Yet, in that moment, I overcame my fear. I managed to do what was necessary, albeit with great trepidation.

These memories, though seemingly trivial, have remained with me. They symbolize the resilience and courage I cultivated from a young age, qualities that have since become a driving force in my life.

WHOLE FAMILY SHELTERING IN ONE ROOM IN DAEBONG-DONG, DAEGU

After our return to Korea, my family settled in Daebong-dong, Jung-gu, Daegu. Our home was near Bangcheon Market in Daebong-dong, close to what is now known as the Kim Gwang-seok Story House (Kim Gwang-seok is a legendary singer songwriter, born and raised in Daegu), with Suseongcheon Stream flowing nearby. The area across Suseongcheon, once a rice field, is now the bustling center of Suseong-gu. We chose this location because it was where my maternal grandfather lived. Although my father's original hometown was Chilgok, no close relatives resided there at the time, prompting his decision to settle in Daegu.

My father supported our family by running a rice shop in Bangcheon Market. He built a small house adjoining the shop, which had only one room and a kitchen. In this humble abode, my mother gave birth to four more children, making us a family of six siblings

– four boys and two girls. Being the eldest, and with a significant 12-year age gap between me and my youngest brother, I shouldered a heavy sense of responsibility from a young age.

The single-room house, with its modest kitchen, soon became cramped for our family of eight. To alleviate this, my father ingeniously added an attic, which naturally became my sleeping area as the eldest son.

I went to elementary, junior high, and senior high schools while living in this house. During my years in this house, I attended Samdeok Elementary School in the adjacent Samdeok-dong. The school was about 2 kilometers away, and I remember the daily 30 to 40-minute walks to and from school. After school, I would play in the neighborhood with rocks or play folded paper toys called "Ddakji". With Suseongcheon nearby, my friends and I often swam in the stream. On one occasion, while preparing to dive into the water from a higher bank, I was suddenly reminded of the fear I had experienced climbing the ferry stairs on our journey to Korea. Despite the fear and the realization that my parents couldn't help me if I fell, I recall diving straight in.

During my elementary school years, my grades weren't top-tier, but a remarkable shift occurred upon entering middle school. From that point, I consistently ranked first or second in the entire school. This academic excellence continued at Gyeongbuk High School, solidifying my reputation as a model student, recognized not only at home but also throughout the market neighborhood.

THE KOREAN WAR AND THE DISCOVERY OF SUPER INTUITION WITHIN ME

The Korean War broke out when I was twelve, forcing my family to evacuate. We sought refuge in Gyeongsan, where my maternal grandparents owned an orchard. With bags packed, my parents led their six children, including myself, away from the war-torn area. One particularly challenging part of our journey was crossing Gomoryeong Hill. The hardship of that experience is vividly recalled whenever I hear the lyrics of 'Rainy Day in Gomoryeong.' The lines, "When will I pass over the hill in the rain, how many hills do I have to pass in life with tears in my eyes?" resonate deeply with me, bringing back poignant memories of my mother's struggle to overcome that hill.

We finally arrived at my grandmother's house, where our family began life as refugees. One Lunar New Year's Day a significant incident occurred. My uncle was preparing to visit a friend's house but couldn't find his ankle bands, despite a thorough search. Pressed for time, he eventually left the house without them. Shortly after his departure, the ankle bands were found. I was a teenager then, and my grandmother asked me to quickly run after my uncle to deliver the bands to him. He had left some time ago, and I wasn't sure if I could catch up, but I started running regardless.

Between us was a river, and people were crossing it using a ferry. If my uncle had already crossed the river, it seemed unlikely that I'd be able to hand him the bands. As I ran down a sloping hill near the river, I spotted my uncle just about to board the ferry. Realizing I was too far to reach him in time, I suddenly noticed I was standing on a bed of pebbles. Acting swiftly, I picked up a pebble, tied it to the bands, and called out, "Uncle!" He heard my shout and turned around just as I threw the pebble with all my strength towards him. Miraculously, I managed to deliver the ankle bands to my uncle just in the nick of time. From a distance, he gestured his thanks.

The quickness of my response in that situation surprised even me. I was amazed at my own ingenuity in coming up with such a solution. Had I not thought to tie the pebble to the ankle bands, I wouldn't have been able to deliver them to my uncle. That incident marked the first time I recognized the intuition within me, an insight that proved useful on many other occasions.

Intuition is the ability to understand something immediately, without the need for conscious reasoning. It's a powerful tool, especially in sudden situations or crises. This skill enables me to quickly find solutions to problems as they arise. It's like my mind works as a computer, rapidly processing information and arriving at an answer. For example, when planning a trip to the United States, I can effortlessly map out my preparations, schedule my time in Seoul, and determine the best route to the airport. Harnessing this intuition can be immensely beneficial in navigating the complex journey of life. It's a skill that, when developed, can offer significant advantages in various situations.

A GOOD STUDENT WITH TOP GRADES

In and around Daebong-dong, my name, Chang Seil, was well-known as that of a student who consistently achieved top grades. I was in my second year of middle school when this particular incident occurred during a class picnic. Back then, students would travel to outings or picnics on foot. As we were passing the road behind my house, our teacher, nicknamed 'Toad,' suddenly stopped us and announced, "This is where Chang Seil lives!" I was taken aback and felt my face flush with embarrassment. Later, I learned that the teacher's intention was to highlight my academic success despite coming from a modest background. At that time, I consistently ranked at the top or second in my class, and even within the entire school, I was always among the top three in terms of grades.

However, my journey as a student wasn't always smooth. As an elementary student, I struggled to grasp even the basic concepts of

My days when I was in junior and senior high schools

My days after graduating college and working for the oil company

addition and subtraction, which naturally resulted in poor grades. It was then that my aunt intervened, patiently teaching me the fundamentals. "You have one here, and you have another one here. When you put them together, you have two. That's addition. And if you take one away, you're left with one. That's subtraction." It was through her guidance that I finally understood these concepts. From then on, my interest in studies grew. A particularly influential figure was my third-grade homeroom teacher, Ms. Lee Hye-sook. Her kind treatment and approachable demeanor made a lasting impression. I remember her as a teacher with a beautiful face and a very pleasant personality.

When I was learning to write, my initial attempts were more like scribbling. However, I was encouraged to improve this habit and practiced diligently until my handwriting was clear and even earned compliments for its neatness. As I progressed to the 3rd and 4th grades, my academic performance improved significantly, and I remember my grades rising to the top ten in my class just before entering middle school.

I recall an incident from when I was in the second grade of elementary school. I had taken money from my mother's purse to buy candy and snacks. Naturally, she discovered this and disciplined me for the act. She used a bamboo strainer for this purpose, and I remember that she hit me so hard that she injured her own hand. This experience was impactful, and I never repeated the offense. Back in the day, parents often employed strict disciplinary measures.

However, it's worth noting that parenting styles have changed over time. In the present day, many parents, perhaps due to having fewer children, seem less inclined to use such methods. This shift raises questions about the balance between discipline and guidance in parenting, because it is the parents' fault if children become unruly due to the lack of discipline.

DOWNFALL OF THE FAMILY
A TOUGH MOTHER AND A TENDER FATHER

My father's rice store was initially thriving. He had successfully saved enough money to take over a neighboring store, thereby expanding his business. However, during this period, a significant civil engineering project was underway to replace a frail wooden bridge over Suseong Stream with a more robust structure. The construction, which lasted four months, was managed by someone close to my father. My father had supplied rice on credit to the construction crew, believing in the project's success. Unfortunately, the construction company declared bankruptcy, resulting in a substantial financial loss for my father. This event marked a turning point for our family.

Following this setback, my father, a kind-hearted and gentle man, was deeply affected. He had a short stature and a handsome face, and was known for his honesty and compassion. However, the loss seemed to overwhelm him, leading to a period where he coped with the stress through excessive drinking. Reflecting on his nature, it's apparent that he was not innately cut out for the ruthless aspects of business. He possessed a gentle demeanor, which, in the competitive world of business, often put him at a disadvantage. As a result, his foray into business was fraught with challenges.

Fortunately, my mother's disposition was quite different from my father's. She was a resilient woman, and in times of crisis, she would inspire and motivate us instead of succumbing to worry. With my father incapacitated by his drinking habits, my mother took control of the business. However, as the saying goes, misfortunes often come in pairs, and this seemed to be the case for us. My mother encountered a significant setback herself. She had been saving money through a 'gye,' a traditional Korean communal fund where members contribute a set amount monthly and take turns receiving the total sum. Tragically, the person managing my mother's gye absconded with the funds. There were ten members in her gye, each contributing one million won per month, aiming to save a total of 10 million won. Being a close-knit group, the betrayal was as painful emotionally as it was financially devastating.

Nevertheless, my mother faced this adversity with remarkable fortitude. Her strength was further evident when I was admitted to Seoul National University. She learned that the woman who had defrauded the gye was running a business in Miari Market in Seoul. I followed rumors about her whereabouts to locate her. I went to the market and located the store run by the woman and her husband. Confronting them, they expressed regret and admitted their inability to repay the full amount, having spent the money. However, perhaps feeling a sense of guilt, they agreed to pay for my college tuition once.

During this period, our family's financial situation deteriorated significantly due to the struggling business. Reflecting on those times, I am often moved to tears by the memory of how my mother single-handedly supported her six children through such hardships. These events unfolded during my middle and high school years, leaving me with serious concerns about my future as I prepared to start college.

CONCERNS OF THE ELDEST SON

As is often the case with children from families that own businesses, I worked to help my parents with their rice store as the eldest son. This sometimes involved delivering rice to customers on a bike. I continued this work until middle school, but once I became recognized as a top student, my mother stopped me from coming to the store after I entered high school. This decision reflected my parents' desire for me to focus solely on my studies, dedicating myself to maintaining good grades.

I had no doubts about attending college, given my strong academic performance before our family's financial situation worsened. My reputation as a model student with top grades was well-known throughout the neighborhood, and even my friends respected me, ensuring we got along well. There's a saying that 'you are where you stand,' and this was true in my case. Despite spending time with friends, swimming in Suseongcheon Stream, I endeavored to uphold the standards of a model student. I steered clear of fights and always strived to be a well-behaved kid.

Meanwhile, as my family's financial situation continued to deteriorate, I began to worry about whether I could afford to go to college. With many younger siblings, a father who was frequently drunk, and a mother shouldering the entire burden alone, I questioned the morality of pursuing higher education. As the eldest son, I felt a strong obligation to contribute to the family's welfare. I contemplated forgoing college to start working and support my siblings.

However, my academic performance at that time was exceptional. I was a student at Gyeongbuk High School in Daegu, a prestigious school where only the top students from junior high schools were admitted. There, I ranked among the top ten students in the entire school. My grades were more than sufficient for admission to Seoul National University, a fact well-known even to the local market vendors, who all assumed I would attend.

Faced with this dilemma, I questioned whether I should abandon my college aspirations to start earning money. I knew, however, that this decision would likely disappoint my mother. Moreover, even if I wanted to work immediately after graduation, the availability of decent jobs for someone in my situation was limited. I was torn and deeply troubled by this decision.

Ultimately, I resolved to pursue a college education. Yet, the

Fortunately, my mother's disposition was quite different from my father's. She was a resilient woman, and in times of crisis, she would inspire and motivate us instead of succumbing to worry. Reflecting on those times, I am often moved to tears by the memory of how my mother single-handedly supported her six children through such hardships.

thought of the tuition fees made me waver again. At that time, my family was in no position to support my college expenses.

THE GRAND DREAM OF
A PRESIDENT AND A JUDGE

When I was in elementary school, I harbored a vague dream of becoming president. This aspiration might have stemmed from my admiration for the then-president, Rhee Syng-man, or perhaps from a desire to hold a position of power. I wasn't alone in this ambition: many of my peers also aspired to become presidents or generals. However, nowadays, I rarely encounter children who express a desire to make that their life's aim. Instead, the common dream among today's youth seems to be becoming popular athletes or celebrities, professions perceived as lucrative. This shift makes me ponder the reasons behind it and leads me to feel a certain sadness about our society's increasing materialism. The frequent portrayal of presidents and politicians in the media, often in the context of mistakes and wrongdoings, might have contributed to this change in perception. In any case, the notion that our lives' purpose is solely for personal prosperity needs to be reevaluated. The ideals encapsulated in the National Charter of Education resonate with me deeply:

'We were born on this land with the historical mission to revive our nation. Internally, it is time to establish independence, and externally, to contribute to the co-prosperity of humanity.'

The clear purpose of our personal lives should be to use them for the betterment of society and our country. For the past 80 years, I have dedicated my life to this purpose. When one lives this way, life becomes more dynamic, and genuine happiness can be experienced. However, a life focused solely on personal prosperity may offer temporary happiness, but ultimately, it fosters mutual hostility, unending greed, and leads to destruction.

When I was in middle school, I unexpectedly came across a law magazine. How a legal magazine ended up in our modest home, a place where we eked out a living by selling rice, remains a mystery to me. Legal terminology is notoriously difficult and often incomprehensible, so one would expect the magazine to be quite uninteresting. However, surprisingly, I found myself captivated by its articles and read them repeatedly. I began to think that becoming a judge, a position of power, could be a steppingstone towards my dream of becoming president. My grades were strong, and I believed they could potentially qualify me for the bar exam and a future career as a judge. This aspiration persisted throughout middle and high school. However, as a high school junior, I gradually abandoned this dream, primarily due to the significant deterioration of my family's financial situation. Being the eldest of six children, I felt an overwhelming responsibility to contribute to my family's support.

CHOOSING BETWEEN THE KOREAN MILITARY ACADEMY AND SEOUL NATIONAL UNIVERSITY COLLEGE OF ENGINEERING

During the winter break of my second year in high school, an event occurred that would significantly influence my future. At that time, the College of Engineering at Seoul National University was highly esteemed. One day, alumni who had graduated from our high school and were then studying at this college visited. They impressed upon us that as capable students, we should aim for the College of Engineering, not only to contribute to our country's industrial development but also to secure a lucrative career. It was the late 1950s, and Korea was experiencing severe poverty, evident even in global economic rankings.

Given my family's declining financial situation and our struggle with poverty, their words resonated with me deeply. I felt compelled to follow this path and expressed my intention to apply to the College of Engineering. However, almost immediately after declaring this, I began to doubt my decision. I questioned whether pursuing engineering alone would allow me to realize my ambitious dream of becoming the president.

Consequently, I considered applying to the Military Academy first, before attempting the entrance exam for the College of Engineering. Although the College of Engineering at Seoul National University did not fully align with my aspirations and presented tuition challenges, the Military Academy seemed more conducive to my dream. Furthermore, as it was fully funded by the government, tuition would not be a concern.

With that plan in mind, I took a train to Seoul for the first time in my life. Nowadays, trains are considered a convenient mode of transportation, but back then, they were in extremely poor condition. Unsurprisingly, there were no seats available. The cars were packed with students like me, all heading to Seoul to take college entrance exams. I observed their school uniforms, and I noticed they were representing various high schools such as Busan High School, Gyeongnam High School, Gyeongnam Girls' High School, and Gyeongbuk Girls' High School. As I stood cramped among them, trying to maintain my balance, a female student from Gyeongbuk Girls' High School considerately shifted to give me a bit more space. I was very grateful for this gesture, but at that time, I was too shy to express my thanks.

As planned, my first stop was to take the exam for the military academy. I believed that the military academy would offer a better opportunity to fulfill my dream. Additionally, I thought that becoming a military officer would enable me to support my family. However, I took the exam while still undecided about which school I would ultimately choose.

The exam to enter the military academy was exceptionally challenging. The math section was comprised of 20 subjective questions, the difficulty of which would be considered extraordinary by today's standards. However, confident in my math skills, I found myself able to solve the problems with ease. For the English test, an interviewer entered the room, opened an English edition of the Digest magazine, and asked me to read it before posing several questions. My confidence in English helped me to answer all the questions correctly.

During the interview, I was asked why I wanted to join the military academy. I candidly shared everything, including my family's situation and my deliberation between Seoul National University's College of Engineering and the Korea Military Academy. Surprisingly, the interviewer, who appeared to be a Seoul National University alumnus and a military officer, recommended that I opt for Seoul National University instead. This conversation ultimately helped me finalize my decision to apply to Seoul National University, resolving my confusion.

Following the interviewer's advice, I sat for the entrance exam at Seoul National University's College of Engineering. This exam was as equally demanding as the military academy's, but I did my utmost to solve each problem. At that time, exam results were announced on the radio. Listening with bated breath, I heard my name and number being called out, marking my successful admission to the College of Engineering at Seoul National University. My parents were overjoyed, declaring it an honor for our family. Yet, amidst this joy, I remained concerned about how we would manage the tuition fees.

WHY I ALMOST THREW UP AFTER EATING MEAT

I remember being tempted to apply to the College of Engineering when Seoul National University students visited our high school. They mentioned the lucrative prospects of studying engineering. This was during the end of Rhee Syng-man's administration, a time when Korea was steeped in poverty. My family, owning a rice business, had access to rice, but most families couldn't afford it. The typical side dishes were limited to kimchi and doenjang, fermented soybean paste. Meat was an unimaginable luxury for most.

Growing up, meat was not part of my diet, which probably explains why I couldn't digest it well. In elementary, middle, and high school, meat appeared on our table only after being used for ancestral rites, and even then, it wasn't meant for the children. Later, while in college, I tutored for a family whose parents hailed from Pyongyang. The father was unemployed, and the mother worked as a dentist. They were fond of meat and often enjoyed grilled meat over charcoal. Once, they offered me some, but after eating it, I experienced stomach upset and almost vomited.

This unpleasant experience made me averse to meat. Even after I started working, during company dinners where meat was served, I would stick to vegetable side dishes and avoid the meat.

There was a time when I went to the Ulsan factory for fieldwork. A colleague there recommended a well-known steak house in the city and invited me to dine out. It wasn't a situation where I could politely decline, so I accompanied him. As we headed to the steak house, I planned to simply avoid eating meat. However, my friend persistently urged me to try it, praising the quality of the steak. Eventually, I gave in to his insistence and tentatively tasted one or two pieces. As expected, the meat unsettled my stomach. While my friend savored his meal, I could only watch and offer a forced smile.

Back then, my dietary limitations weren't just confined to meat; I also couldn't stomach raw fish or sushi. Once, a friend invited me for sushi, and I agreed to go. While he relished every bite, I found myself unable to even taste the sushi, simply watching him enjoy the meal.

Later, while working at the Ulsan factory, I gradually began to incorporate meat into my diet. The field workers often ate meat, and I felt it was necessary to adapt to their eating habits to fit in. Slowly, I started to consume meat more regularly. However, it wasn't until my 40s that I became comfortable with eating meat. Until then, my diet was predominantly vegetarian.

I talked about my experience with meat to highlight how each person has one or two weaknesses. Often, people find themselves living lives constrained by these weaknesses. If you do not address and resolve these issues, you are likely to live a life uncomfortably shackled by your weaknesses. However, overcoming them releases you from these bonds, allowing you to live more freely. In this context, my incident with meat helped me realize that weaknesses are not there to torment us, but rather to be conquered. I encourage you, too, not to become a slave to your weaknesses but to live a life dedicated to overcoming them.

MAKING MONEY AS A TUTOR WHILE STUDYING IN COLLEGE
WHAT I LEARNED WHILE BEING A LIVE-IN TUTOR

Even now, there persists a culture that regards admission to Seoul National University as an honor for the family, the school, and the region, and some people even put up a poster to announce a student's admission to the prestigious college. Back then, as it is now, gaining admission to Seoul National University was a significant achievement. Consequently, I hoped that my relatively well-to-do maternal uncle and aunt would help with my tuition. However, as the tuition due date neared, I heard nothing from them. In the end, the woman who had previously taken my mother's money and fled, as I mentioned earlier, was the one who paid my first semester's tuition. This experience left me with a lasting grievance towards my maternal relatives. Years later, when I met my aunt, she apologized for not contributing at that time. I accepted her apology, acknowledging that the experience had ultimately made me stronger.

That's how my college life at Seoul National University College of Engineering began. Back then, the college was located in Gongneung, giving it a rural feel. I lived in a boarding house near the campus, barely managing my first year with the money my parents sent. Being the eldest son, fully aware of my family's financial struggles, I felt a constant burden. Then, during my freshman year's winter break, I received a letter from my younger brother. It detailed our family's difficulties, and I couldn't finish reading it without tears. It was at that moment I decided to find a tutoring job to earn my own money.

At that time, many of my friends from poor families at Seoul National University were earning money as live-in tutors. I inquired about how to find such a tutoring job, and they advised me to place an advertisement in a newspaper. It only cost a few dollars to do so, and eventually, I secured a live-in tutoring position for a family in Chungjeong-ro, Seodaemun. I tutored two children in the family: a junior-high boy preparing for high school and an elementary school girl getting ready for junior high. I dedicated myself to tutoring them, and thankfully, they both were admitted to the schools they had applied to. I remember that they had a grandmother who couldn't praise me enough.

The family was so fond of me that once, the children's aunt approached me with a proposal for me to marry her daughter. She wanted to arrange a meeting, but I declined, explaining that I was only a sophomore in college and not ready to consider marriage.

However, she persisted, and her husband, an employee at Korea Electric Power Corporation, better known as KEPCO also took a liking to me after meeting me. Consequently, I agreed to meet their daughter, but I didn't feel a connection at first, so the matter ended after that initial meeting.

In December of my sophomore year in college, the family I was tutoring for encountered a problem: The father, who worked as a second secretary at the U.S. Embassy, had to resign unexpectedly and stay at home. Consequently, I had to leave and find another live-in tutoring job.

My next position was in Ojang-dong, Euljiro. By then, I was a junior in college and had applied to join the ROTC team. As I needed to participate in training, I feared the family might not hire me if they knew, so I started tutoring without disclosing this. The ROTC training was scheduled for the summer break in August, and as it drew closer, I could no longer keep it a secret. After informing the family, the father, originally from the North, appeared bewildered. Upon returning after the training month, I discovered that they had replaced me with another tutor, which meant I had to search for yet another position.

My third tutoring job was with a dentist's family in Yongsan. The husband was unemployed, and his wife, the dentist, asked me to tutor their high school senior son who aspired to attend Seoul National University. This position was short-lived since the son was nearing the end of high school and my services were only required until his graduation. After this, I moved to Yeongdeungpo and Cheongpa-dong, spending the rest of my senior year as a live-in tutor. A notable incident from this time occurred when I was battling a severe cold as a junior transitioning to senior year. A Navy colonel, who frequently visited the family, gave me some medicine. Remarkably, it cured me so effectively that I felt as if I had never been ill. I was deeply grateful to him then, and I extend my thanks again, should he ever read this book.

Undertaking live-in tutoring inevitably comes with time constraints that can impede full dedication to college studies. Daily, several hours were spent tutoring the student, and about four hours were lost commuting between the student's home and the campus in Gongneung. Despite these challenges, I am grateful for the live-in tutoring opportunity, as it allowed me to complete college without financially burdening my mother. However, I do regret not being able to fully immerse myself in college life.

Through live-in tutoring, I learned valuable lessons beyond academic knowledge. While school studies are theoretical, live-in tutoring provided practical experience learning. The ultimate goal of education is to excel in social life, and in this context, skills in one's field are as crucial as adeptness in interpersonal relationships. Many professionals today attribute workplace challenges to difficulties in that area. In this respect, it's fair to say that my early experiences with live-in tutoring were instrumental in teaching me about human relationships. The families who entrusted me with tutoring were, in a sense, my customers. Working for various families, I learned how to engage with these 'customers,' and this experience became a foundational asset in my later professional and business endeavors. Additionally, the financial aspect of this arrangement was advantageous; I earned while learning, as opposed to paying for education like most students. What could be more rewarding than that?

CHAPTER 4

SADE LEARNED FROM LIFE

LESSONS ABOUT SMALL DETAILS

APPLYING FOR ROTC AND THE TRAINING FROM HELL

Even during my college years, I constantly thought hard about achieving success and helping my family improve their situation. In search of opportunities, I learned that joining the military as an ROTC (Reserve Officers' Training Corps) officer would reduce my mandatory service to two years, compared to the three-year requirement for ordinary soldiers. Additionally, becoming an ROTC officer meant receiving a lieutenant's salary, which would provide financial support during my service. This prospect intrigued me.

I decided to join the ROTC team, took the required test, and passed. The ROTC program mandated group training for one month each August during the junior and senior years of college. At that time, I was primarily supporting myself as a live-in tutor, so taking a month off for training presented a significant challenge.

Applying for ROTC and the training from hell

However, the benefits of being on the ROTC team were too valuable to forego.

When summer break arrived, I commenced my ROTC training in August. The training for Seoul National University's ROTC group was mainly conducted at the 30th Division Search Unit. As a college student unfamiliar with military life, I approached the training as though it were a mere camping trip. But the moment I set foot on the training ground I encountered an intense atmosphere. The instructors and teaching assistants began to rigorously discipline us as soon as we arrived, akin to cats intimidating rats. It was then that we fully realized the seriousness and uniqueness of the situation we had entered.

August is the hottest month of the year. The tropical nights made it impossible to sleep until dawn, but we were required to rise from bed without fail at 6 a.m. each morning. The instructors gave us no respite from the moment we got up until 10 p.m. I had hoped for a brief break after dinner, but I was mistaken. Once darkness fell, it was time for night training.

Our barracks housed 40 people, and we were to be in bed by 10 p.m., with two individuals standing guard each hour. With 16 people taking turns over the span of eight hours, from ten at night until six in the morning, each of us in the barracks had to stand guard once every two days. Waking up at dawn inevitably led to sleep deprivation. Consequently, I rarely had a good night's sleep throughout the entire training period.

Furthermore, the instructors were unyielding in enforcing military discipline. If even one person was late for the morning muster, the entire group had to start over from the beginning. The same rule applied to meal times. Any latecomer would result in disciplinary action for the entire group. Therefore, all 40 of us had to move in unison, without exception. Only after all 40 members successfully passed this initial stage of discipline were we allowed to proceed to the training ground for further training. That was when the truly grueling part of the training commenced.

We underwent rigorous training sessions, including parachute landing fall practices and night exercises, all in the scorching heat. The search team's parachute landing fall training is notoriously intense, often pushing human limits. Through these demanding exercises, we gradually transformed from romantically-inclined college students into soldiers instilled with strict military discipline.

After completing this strenuous training, I returned to the house where I had been a live-in tutor, only to discover that someone else had taken over my role. This was somewhat expected. My student's father told me he was sorry, but I couldn't shake off the feeling of dejection. There I was, in the middle of Seoul, with nowhere to go. Fortunately, I had a friend attending Seoul National University's College of Education. I reached out to him, and he kindly took me out to dinner. It was a relief to be able to share my experiences from the month-long training and express my feelings about losing the tutoring job.

RETURNING HOME AS A COMMISSIONED OFFICER

Finally, after completing my ROTC training, I was commissioned as a second lieutenant. I was assigned to serve in the Army Signal School. Before commencing my duties there, I decided to visit my parents, donning my military uniform. However, upon arriving home, I was confronted with the dire situation my family was facing. They were grappling with the aftermath of my father's credit transaction incident and the financial loss from my mother's earlier financial ordeal.

Consequently, my parents had lost enough money to be evicted from their rice shop and were forced to move to Bongdeok-dong, on the southern outskirts of Daegu. They didn't even have a proper house to live in; instead, they were residing in a makeshift shanty constructed on an empty lot. My parents had managed to partition this humble dwelling into two rooms to accommodate their children. My mother was barely making ends meet by working as a vendor at Bongdeok Market.

I only became aware of the full extent of these hardships when I visited my family for the first time during the last school break. As the eldest son, the reality of their situation weighed heavily on me. All I could think of was achieving success as quickly as possible to help my family regain stability.

And then, before returning to the military, I visited home again and witnessed a distressing scene. Workers from Daegu City Hall were digging up the ground next to my family's shanty with pickaxes. It turned out they were there to demolish the shanty, as it was an unlicensed structure. My mother and siblings stood by, crying profusely. My heart sank, and tears uncontrollably started to pour. The world seemed to be crumbling before me, and I felt utterly helpless. I stood there, staring blankly at the scene, as if in a daze, and then, with tears in my eyes, I turned and left home without uttering a word.

I started my duties at the Army Signal School with the heavy thought that my family's home had been demolished. I believed that the only way to alleviate my family's misfortune was to achieve success quickly. So, I dedicated myself to my military duties, eagerly awaiting the passage of time. About a year later, I finally received news from home. To my astonishment, the shanty had not been demolished. I learned that the local town chief had intervened, pleading with the city hall workers: "The son of this family graduated from Seoul National University. He's incredibly bright. Please, do this family a favor and leave them be. Your kindness will be repaid in the future." Upon hearing this, the workers left without demolishing the shanty.

I cannot express how grateful I was upon hearing this story. I shuddered to think what might have happened to my mother, father, and younger siblings if the house had been destroyed. This incident renewed my determination to succeed, as I cried and clenched my fists with resolve.

The neighborhood where we lived in an unlicensed structure condemned to be demolished. As of 2022 in the photo

FIRST MILITARY SERVICE AT THE ARMY SIGNAL SCHOOL
THE TIME I DISCOVERED THE LAW OF SMALL DETAILS

After completing three months of training at the Army Signal School in Daejeon, I began my official military service as a communications officer instructor at the school. This role marked the start of my real military service.

Communications officer instructors teach various subjects. Among these, the radar course was considered the most advanced. It required instructors to possess sophisticated electronic skills to train signal soldiers in operating and maintaining radar-related equipment. Due to our high-level knowledge in electronic technology, several graduates from Seoul National University College of Engineering, including myself, were assigned to teach this course.

Radar technology, especially at that time, was one of the most complex pieces of military equipment. While modern radars consist of transistors, the radars then were made up of hundreds of thousands of vacuum tubes. These tubes formed tightly connected circuits through which electric current flowed. Understanding the workings of just one tube was insufficient to grasp the entire system. I realized that only by comprehending all the physical reactions occurring within the system could one fully understand and apply this knowledge elsewhere. In this sense, serving as a radar course instructor was a pivotal point in my study of details.

Several engineering college graduates were also undergoing training at the Army Signal School. After the training concluded, most were assigned to various locations, leaving only two or three, as far as I remember, to continue teaching the radar course at the signal school. This select group of graduates, including myself, was tasked with the responsibility of instructing the radar course.

During my time as an instructor, I had the opportunity to engage in advanced studies within the communications department. This period allowed me to read extensively, a variety of books, including those in English and Japanese. As a result, I gained access to electrical knowledge beyond what I had learned in college. On one occasion, a major handed me an English-language electronics dictionary and requested that I translate it. I completed the translation, and he was highly impressed. It turned out that he had asked several other instructors to do the same, but he considered my translation to be the best. As a token of appreciation for my work, he rewarded me with 1,000 won. While this sum might not have been significant for him, given that his salary was 100,000 won, it was a substantial

The radar installations then were made up of hundreds of thousands of vacuum tubes. These tubes formed tightly connected circuits through which electric current flowed. Understanding the workings of just one tube was insufficient to grasp the entire system. I realized that only by comprehending all the physical reactions occurring within the system could one fully understand and apply this knowledge elsewhere. In this sense, serving as a radar course instructor was a pivotal point in my study of details.

amount for me. I was thrilled and deeply moved by this gesture of recognition.

At the time, my monthly salary was 4,600 won, making the 1,000 won reward over 20% of my monthly pay. From my salary, I sent 2,000 won to my younger sister in Daegu. Additionally, I had to pay 1,600 won for room and board, as officers were not permitted to stay and dine at the signal school facilities. Consequently, I lived in a boarding house near the school. After these expenses, I was left with 900 won, which I used to purchase books and cover transportation costs.

The principal of the Army Signal School, a two-star general, took a particular liking to me. He assigned us the task of writing about rocket launching. My submission, which utilized all the knowledge I acquired in college and was completed after diligent research, seemed to impress him greatly.

This experience during my military service was particularly meaningful as it allowed me to be acknowledged for my capabilities. It was a moment that confirmed the existence of abilities within me that I hadn't recognized before. After completing my one-year duty at the signal school, I received an assignment to a front-line unit, which required me to travel a considerable distance.

PRACTICAL EXPERIENCE LEARNED WHILE BEING SIGNAL COMMANDER FOR A FRONTLINE UNIT

Initially, I was mentally prepared for a transfer after completing my one-year tenure at the signal school. I had expected to be assigned to division headquarters, considering my capabilities had been recognized there. However, to my surprise, I was ordered to move to a battalion-level frontline unit. Initially, I felt a bit disappointed, but I soon saw it as a beneficial opportunity. Eager to gain real field experience, I headed to my new post with a relatively relaxed mindset.

My assignment was as the head of the signal company of the 1st Battalion, 8th Division, located in Jeongok, Yeoncheon-gun, Gyeonggi province. Contrary to the belief that frontline units involved little training and activity, my first encounter with the battalion commander was quite intense. When I reported to his barracks, the atmosphere was so intimidating that other officers hardly dared to raise their heads, and the commander himself was dismissive, barely acknowledging me. It seemed like an intentional effort to intimidate me right from the start. I later learned that I was not the only one who had received such treatment from this commander and was advised to be cautious.

About a week later, the commander called me in and demanded that I fix a broken amplifier. I informed him that I would inspect it, prepare a list of the necessary parts, and submit it to the operations department. After organizing the list, I passed it to the operations department. However, the commander soon confronted me, angrily questioning why I hadn't fixed the amplifier. It was then I realized his expectations. I told him I would take it offsite for repairs and left for Seoul, leaving the amplifier at a radio repair shop. Unfortunately, even the repair shop couldn't fix it, so I returned it as is and reported back to the commander. To my surprise, he grinned and patted me on the back, signaling his approval. It dawned on me that all this had been a test by the commander, likely stemming from an inferiority complex upon learning that I was a Seoul National University graduate and former instructor at the Army Signal School.

Afterward, I was selected for nuclear energy training at the regiment and graduated as the top student. This achievement brought honor to the battalion and even afforded the battalion commander an opportunity to receive training at the ROK Army College. Subsequently, the battalion commander was replaced, and the new commander took a liking to me and placed great trust in my abilities. A month later, our unit was suddenly relocated to Pocheon. From my perspective, this move was beneficial, as rear units like ours in Pocheon typically had more training opportunities, allowing me more chances to showcase my skills.

As expected, the rear unit in Pocheon had more extensive training than frontline units, and my role as the signal commander became more demanding. My duty included advancing to the training location to set up the entire communications system in preparation for the incoming troops. While this task might seem straightforward, it was far from simple. A company consisted of 250 to 300 troops, and a battalion comprised about four such companies. This meant I was responsible for the communication systems supporting the movement of up to 1,000 troops.

During training, battalion commanders, company commanders, and platoon commanders needed to move around and maintain constant communication, making it challenging to avoid any disruptions. While things generally went smoothly, any communication failure could have serious consequences. In fact, one of my peers was sent to jail due to a communication breakdown during training.

When a training order was issued, the first step involved meticulously reviewing the training map. It was crucial to identify the locations of the 1st Battalion headquarters, the 1st, 2nd, and 3rd Companies, and the Headquarters Company, both on the map and in the actual terrain. Accurately interpreting the terrain was paramount, as often there are discrepancies between the map and reality.

A single peak on the map, for example, could correspond to as many as four peaks in reality. However, understanding the terrain wasn't enough; weather conditions also played a vital role in our planning. Once these factors were assessed, we could then proceed to set up a wired communication network accordingly.

The communication team's role was also critical during the withdrawal phase post-training. It was essential that the team be capable of quickly and efficiently dismantling the communication facilities after all training units had departed. I imparted this practical training to the 30 soldiers under my command, ensuring they could not only learn but also effectively execute these tasks. Thanks to our thorough preparation, the signal soldiers I supervised successfully completed their mission, and our unit managed to conclude the training without any incidents. This success brought me immense satisfaction, as my abilities as a communications commander were recognized by many.

No matter how skilled one is, divine intervention plays a role in preventing mishaps. A single error by any of the communication soldiers could have led to an accident. However, I believe that our flawless execution was not only a testament to our abilities but also a blessing from above. From that moment on, I began to feel a deep sense of gratitude towards heaven.

Afterward, I was discharged from the military in March 1965, exactly two years after enlisting in March 1963, and reentered civilian life. My military service lasted only two years, but in retrospect, it was a period filled with truly eventful experiences. Despite facing many complexities, it was a valuable time during which I learned a great deal. Like most men who have served in the military, I regard my military experience as an invaluable part of my life that I will never forget.

ONE MONTH OF HARSH EXPERIENCE IN MY FIRST JOB

Immediately after my discharge from the military, I went to my school for career counseling, as it was time to seek a real job. While there, a professor approached me with a request: "I have an alumni who owns a business. Would you help him out for just a month?" Feeling obligated, I agreed. I was discharged from the military on March 30th, and I started working at my first job on April 1st.

The company was a manufacturer of cigarette foil. Upon my arrival, I noticed an electrician and several workers in the factory who appeared quite wary of me. The boss's first task for me was to examine and repair the cigarette foil auxiliary paper drying machine, which was malfunctioning. My studies had covered machinery, but only in theory; this was my first encounter with an actual machine. To address the issue, I had to consult reference books.

About 10 days into the job, I was assigned to inspect the automatic facilities in a factory spanning approximately 1,300m2. I observed that the facility consisted of dozens of mechanical and electrical devices, as well as motors, all intricately interconnected and operating automatically. However, the entire system had been installed incorrectly, causing significant malfunctions. The electrician and workers were attempting to dismantle and reinstall everything. My arrival on the first day, coupled with my background as a graduate from the College of Engineering at Seoul National University of Technology, made them apprehensive. They feared that I might replace them, potentially costing them their jobs.

While I was engaged in machine repair work at the company, we experienced a power outage. Despite having only been there for 10 days, I was tasked with resolving this electricity issue. Fixing the power outage required climbing up a utility pole to inspect the electrical equipment. I requested the key to the switchboard breaker and began ascending the ladder. During that one-minute climb, a flurry of thoughts raced through my mind. I felt a sense of disrespect, wondering if they thought this was the type of work I envisioned while studying engineering at a prestigious university like Seoul National University. Upon reaching the top of the pole, fear gripped me. I realized that one wrong move could lead to electrocution, potentially ending my life. Nonetheless, I managed to steady my nerves and locate the disjoined cable, which I then fixed before climbing down.

Only after activating the circuit breaker in the switchboard room did I feel a sense of relief. Those 10 minutes felt like an eternity, oscillating between feelings of dread and relief.

Returning to the substation, I turned on the switch, and the machinery whirred back to life. The sense of accomplishment I felt at that moment was beyond words. It was a satisfaction I would never have experienced if I had let my pride as a Seoul National University graduate prevent me from undertaking the task.

It didn't end there. Next, the mechanical team leader asked me to connect a set of complex control cables. While pondering the intricacies of this task, a sudden inspiration struck me, and I successfully connected the cables without much difficulty. It seemed that the team leader was impressed with my innovative method, as it was something he had never considered before. There was also another challenging issue, which I managed to resolve, further boosting my confidence in my abilities.

Even though it was only a one-month experience in April, I learned a great deal. The factory workers' cautious attitude towards me taught me not to underestimate anything that I would encounter going forward, and I also gained the confidence that I could accomplish anything as long as I faced challenges with courage. This one-month period proved to be an invaluable experience for me, laying a strong foundation for my career.

THE IMPORTANCE OF SMALL DETAILS LEARNED THROUGH LIFE EXPERIENCE

While working the temporary job at the cigarette silver foil manufacturing factory in April, I prepared to take an exam for a position at the Korea National Oil Corporation. At that time, securing a job at this leading public corporation was the dream of every engineering student at Seoul National University. I learned about the corporation's recruitment drive through a newspaper advertisement. Fortunately, the exam was scheduled for a Saturday, so there would be no conflict with my workdays.

Upon arriving at the testing site, I was surprised to see many graduates from Seoul National University's College of Engineering, including alumni who had graduated years earlier and others who were already well-employed. This realization caused my confidence to waver, as I, fresh out of the military, doubted my ability to outperform these experienced and competent applicants. Nonetheless, I resolved to give it my best.

To my astonishment, I passed the exam. The competition was fierce: out of 20 graduates from the Engineering Department, I was the only one who passed. In the Machinery Department, only one out of 20 passed, while in the Civil Engineering Department, only two out of forty succeeded, and from the Chemical Engineering Department, just two out of 20 were accepted. I still believe that a stroke of luck played a significant role in my passing the exam.

The joy of being accepted into Korea National Oil Corporation was indescribable, as it meant I could finally contribute financially to my family's well-being. As the eldest son, I had always felt the pressure to support my family in need. Sharing this news with my parents, who were overjoyed, gave me a profound sense of fulfillment and happiness, almost as if I could fly.

I began working at Korea National Oil Corporation in May 1965. Having been discharged from the military in March and worked at the silver foil factory in April, I transitioned smoothly into my new career without any gaps.

My role was in the technical department at the Korea National Oil Corporation headquarters. At the time, the corporation was operating a plant that imported and refined oil, and my department oversaw the technology related to this operation. However, from my very first day, I noticed a stark difference in the work environment compared to my previous experiences. The oil company had adopt-

Accustomed to the military's directive approach, where I was only expected to follow orders, I initially found this autonomy somewhat bewildering. I struggled at first, unsure of how to proceed in a setting where I was expected to independently identify and undertake tasks. Yet, this autonomous environment eventually prompted me to engage in self-directed learning, which greatly enhanced my on-the-job skills and knowledge.

ed an advanced system, fostering a corporate culture of autonomy among employees. Accustomed to the military's directive approach, where I was only expected to follow orders, I initially found this autonomy somewhat bewildering. I struggled at first, unsure of how to proceed in a setting where I was expected to independently identify and undertake tasks. Yet, this autonomous environment eventually prompted me to engage in self-directed learning, which greatly enhanced my on-the-job skills and knowledge.

A SUBORDINATE WITH SUPERIOR-LEVEL PERFORMANCE
THE RESULT-MAKING POWER OF SMALL DETAILS

The autonomous system at Korea National Oil Corporation greatly facilitated the use of my creativity. Upon joining the corporation, I discovered that most of my superiors were alumni from Seoul National University College of Engineering. However, none of them assigned me specific tasks or provided direct instructions. Initially, this left me confused, and I reached out to my senior manager and contacted colleagues at the Ulsan plant for guidance, but to no avail. Consequently, I decided to take the initiative and began by thoroughly reviewing the company's entire factory layout. This approach proved to be the right choice, as it gave me insights into potential areas of work.

To effectively contribute to the petrochemical plant technology operations, I recognized the need for further study, as my existing academic knowledge was insufficient. I purchased original books in

English and Japanese, diligently read and researched them, and then applied this new knowledge to practical fieldwork. Although I encountered some initial trial and error, my efforts eventually led to steady progress and significant contributions to the company.

The executives at the company were surprised to witness my accomplishments, and so were the heads of partner companies, who praised my performance as exceptional. Despite my performance being reported to my superiors, they remained silent on the matter. Nevertheless, I continued with my work. Before the year was over, I achieved something remarkable: Although I had been with the company for less than a year, I created a comprehensive business plan for the entire company for the upcoming year. This plan outlined the necessary tasks for the company as a whole and the expansion plans for the Ulsan plant facilities.

When drafting such a business plan, attention to detail is crucial. I included specifics on the operation of each engineering machine and electrical facility. Furthermore, determining the budget for these plans was of utmost importance. I meticulously calculated the detailed budget and completed the business proposal.

However, my efforts did not stop there. A business plan, no matter how well-crafted, is merely theoretical unless implemented. Therefore, I also developed an execution plan for realizing the business proposal. I had prepared thoroughly, anticipating that questions regarding the execution of the plan would arise once it was presented to the board of directors. My well-prepared business plan received

I am designing a facility at the Korea National Oil Corporation.

the board's approval, and the following year, I was entrusted with overseeing its implementation. In my second year on the job, I was handling responsibilities typically assigned to managers or directors.

What is crucial in carrying out work is the precise execution of the budget. Having either insufficient or excessive funds can pose problems. The key is to adhere strictly to the budget. Therefore, I created a detailed budget plan, specifying the amount to be spent during the contract stage and each stage going forward. By following the pre-planned execution strategy, we successfully completed the project without any issues.

To ensure the project's success, I made weekly visits to the Ulsan plant despite the challenging transportation conditions of the time. Unlike today, where one can travel to Ulsan and back within a day using the KTX (Korea Train eXpress, Korea's high-speed rail system) or airplanes, back then, it took two days and one night. There was no direct transportation to Ulsan, so I had to take a train to Daegu, then a bus to Gyeongju, and finally from Gyeongju to Ulsan. Usually, I finished my work late at night, necessitating an overnight stay in Ulsan before returning to Seoul via the same route.

My dedication paid off when I was promoted to manager just 2 years and 8 months after joining the company, marking the fastest promotion among my peers who were hired at the same time. My college friends were envious yet congratulatory, and even friends working at POSCO (Pohang Iron and Steel Company, Ltd) called to inquire how I managed such a rapid promotion. At the time, I didn't have an answer. But now, over 50 years later, I can pinpoint the secret: it's the 'details'. Reflecting on my life, I realize the importance of attention to small details was ingrained in me since my childhood in Japan, through my education in elementary, middle, high school, and college, and during my time in the army. The first significant outcome of this focus on details manifested in the business plan I drafted for the Korea National Oil Corporation.

When examining the business plan I developed for Korea National Oil Corporation, one can see that it started with an overview of the company's entire blueprint. In any endeavor, it's crucial to

My colleagues and I at Korea National Oil Corporation after a seminar

first understand the whole picture. Only by looking at the entirety can you identify which parts are functioning well and which are problematic. A system flows smoothly only when all its components are organically connected, and a single malfunctioning part can disrupt the entire process. The question then arises: what causes these malfunctions? The answer lies in the experience I had at the silver foil manufacturing company, where the root cause of the breakdown was inadequate preparation and careless work. It was by focusing on the minor details that I eventually identified and resolved the issue.

Similarly, when crafting the business plan for Korea National Oil Corporation, I made sure to incorporate even the most intricate details. Importantly, these details were not just theoretical concepts formed at a desk; they were based on actual on-site realities and practical considerations.

When you have a well-crafted business plan, its potential for success is often evident at first glance. This is because the level of detail in the plan is a key indicator of its feasibility. If the overall business plan encompasses all necessary details, the likelihood of failure is almost negligible, provided that the plan is executed as designed. This meticulous approach to planning was instrumental in my promotion to manager in just 2 years and 8 months.

In any endeavor, it's crucial to first understand the whole picture. Only by looking at the entirety can you identify which parts are functioning well and which are problematic. A system flows smoothly only when all its components are organically connected, because a single malfunctioning part can disrupt the entire process. The root cause of a breakdown is inadequate preparation and careless work.

DEVOTION TO SADE BUILDS CONFIDENCE AND SKILLS

At that time, I worked alongside colleagues who had graduated from Seoul National University's College of Engineering, some in the same year as me and others in earlier years. When I was promoted first, there were complaints among them that my advancement had impeded their own promotion opportunities. In response, I delegated responsibilities to them, intending to provide them a chance for promotion. However, the feedback I received was often, 'Oh my gosh, it's difficult for us to do this job.' I was initially puzzled by their reluctance. I believed they were smart enough to handle the tasks, yet I often wondered why they struggled to complete them.

Eventually, I realized that those who were unable to finish assigned tasks typically shared a common trait: a pervasive belief that they couldn't do it. The root of this mindset, I discovered, was a lack of skill. This deficiency often stemmed from a reluctance to study and attempt new challenges. When people recognize a skill gap, it's imperative to study and work hard to bridge it. However, my colleagues would often give up before even trying. You cannot expect development and growth when you have this attitude.

Soon after I began working at the company, I was tasked with creating a design. This was a daunting challenge, as I had never drawn a design during my time in school. However, I was determined not to give up. I dedicated myself to learning how to draw until I was able to successfully submit my design.

Devotion to small details starts with the commitment to try your best and persevere instead of giving up. To accomplish what you currently cannot, you need to engage in study. Through this process, you begin to uncover the finer details of the task that were initially elusive. The moment you grasp these small details, you start building your confidence, and eventually, you become capable of fulfilling your responsibilities. These experiences accumulate and evolve into valuable skills. Ultimately, it's important to remember that all human weaknesses and deficiencies in skills are often due to a lack of understanding of the smallest details.

THE FIELD IS THE BEST PLACE TO LEARN SADE

After my promotion to manager, the common reaction I received was, 'You'll be glad that you don't have to go down to Ulsan anymore.' However, as an engineer, I believed that more could be learned in the field than in the office. I harbored a strong desire to leave the office and engage in field work.

I maintained the belief that tasks should be executed by competent individuals and that minimizing costs was crucial for the company's benefit. I viewed the field as the ideal environment to apply these principles and to further develop my engineering skills. At that time, a significant factory construction project was underway in Ulsan, and I was offered an opportunity to work on site. I chose to engage in field work without much hesitation.

When I first joined Korea National Oil Corporation, the company was processing 12,500 barrels of oil per day. During my time

The details I learned in the field laid the groundwork for establishing Ilsung in the future. This detailed knowledge, acquired through field study, significantly elevated my skill level. The field is a better place than office to build skills as an engineer.

there, this capacity doubled to 25,000 barrels, and eventually increased further to 50,000 and then 100,000 barrels. It was a period of rapid and substantial growth for the oil company.

Since the increase in production capacity at Korea National Oil Corporation necessitated the expansion of production facilities, the company was in a constant state of building new factories. My role in this expansion involved constructing all the auxiliary facilities necessary for producing petroleum products. The projects were broadly categorized into the construction of electrical, civil engineering, and machinery-related facilities. Among these, I was specifically tasked with overseeing the electrical-related facilities.

At that time, the headquarters of Korea National Oil Corporation was located in the Hanil Building, situated between Myeongdong and Chungmuro in Seoul. This building was well-known and even featured in a movie of the era. I have fond memories of enjoying delicious meals at nearby Chinese restaurants like Donghaeru and Myeongdong Kalguksu during lunch breaks. I worked at this location for 2 years and 8 months until my promotion to manager. Despite developing a special attachment to the place, I made a bold decision to move to Ulsan, driven by the conviction that the field is the best place to learn details!

The details I learned in the field laid the groundwork for establishing Ilsung in the future. When I was managing factory facilities from an office desk, it was difficult to obtain detailed information about the machinery. However, fieldwork necessitated an in-depth study of machines and metals. During this period, I extensively studied related books, including original texts in foreign languages. Just as people undergo changes with age, so do machines. If left unattended, like a worsening disease, machines also deteriorate over time. The required quality inspections to maintain machines in optimal condition vary depending on the situation. This detailed knowledge, acquired through field study, significantly elevated my skill level.

SUPERVISING THE CONSTRUCTION OF OFFSHORE CRUDE OIL PIPELINES AND OPERATION OF LONG-DISTANCE ONSHORE OIL PIPELINES

At that time, ongoing construction was expanding the petrochemical plant in Ulsan. I was responsible for the overall management and supervision of the construction work. For a young man of only 29 years old, it was challenging to liaise with large construction companies such as Hyundai Engineering & Construction and Hankook Machinery, and to manage and supervise field managers, many of whom were older than me.

When I arrived at the construction site with a heavy sense of responsibility, I immediately sensed the challenges ahead, as I had anticipated. A critical component of the petrochemical plant project involved establishing a facility to receive oil from large oil tankers. However, due to their immense size and weight, these tankers could only navigate up to 2,500 meters from the coast. Consequently, constructing a pipeline from that point to the mainland was essential.

This task, although seemingly straightforward, turned out to be an arduous project that spanned over a year. Typically, welding would be used for piping work on an oil pipeline-laying ship, but in an effort to reduce costs, the work involved pulling the pipeline from the sea to the land. This process would have been feasible for distances of 100 or 200 meters, but we were dealing with distances of 1,000 to 2,000 meters. Pulling the pipeline over such lengths, especially considering the weight of the tanker, proved to be exceptionally challenging. This complexity led to delays in construction and heightened my anxiety about the project's completion. As a result, I dedicated myself fully to the task, starting work at 6 in the morning and continuing until midnight.

Fortunately, after significant effort, we successfully completed the construction. Even now, when I think back, it was an incredibly nerve-wracking experience. That was how my first field assignment unfolded amidst numerous challenges. There were subsequent changes, such as returning to work at the Seoul headquarters after two years in the field. However, when the opportunity for a long-distance oil pipeline construction project arose in 1972, I eagerly applied for field work again. This project was a large-scale undertaking, involving the building of an oil pipeline from Ulsan to Uijeongbu, passing through Daegu, Waegwan, Daejeon, and Seoul.

During this time, the long-distance oil pipeline construction support team had an office in Daegu, where I relocated for work. The Daegu office functioned as a control center for the entire oil pipeline construction, in collaboration with the Eighth US Army Fuels Management Flight, also known as POL (Petroleum, Oils, and Lubricants). At that time, there were two major long-distance oil pipeline projects underway: one line running from Ulsan to Uijeongbu via Daegu, Waegwan, Daejeon, and Seoul, and another line extending from Pohang to Uijeongbu, following the same route through Daegu, Waegwan, Daejeon, and Seoul.

The most critical technology in oil pipeline construction involves transporting refined petroleum products to their destination without mixing them. These products, including high-grade gasoline, regular gasoline, kerosene, and diesel, are separated before entering the pipeline. When pressure is applied, they are designed to move in separated layers towards the destination. However, some mixing can occur at the boundaries of these layers. The mixed portions must be removed and separated again. The Daegu office was responsible for controlling this process. As a representative of the Korea National Oil Corporation, I was involved in planning and establishing these procedures, working alongside the eighty-member U.S. Army fuel management team.

To ensure the success of this oil pipeline project, I undertook a month-long business trip to the United States, a first for me. This experience, which involved touring the oil pipelines of this advanced country, proved to be immensely beneficial. It significantly contributed to the successful execution of Korea's long-distance oil pipeline project.

Currently, when people are offered a choice between office work and field work, it's likely that all of them would opt for the office. This preference is even more pronounced among those from elite backgrounds. However, I chose a different path, believing that more detailed answers are found in the field than in the office. This choice, I believe, was key to Ilsung's global success. But this is not to underestimate the importance of office work. I have considerable experience in office settings myself. The drawback of office work, though, is the lack of field knowledge. The office is where commands are given, while the field is where the actual work happens. Imagine the consequences of commanding without understanding field conditions. If inappropriate orders lead to failures in the field, who bears the responsibility?

I share this to reiterate the significance of understanding both the big picture and the finer details. Office work alone doesn't provide a complete picture of field situations. Therefore, even if your role is primarily office-based, I encourage you to spend time in the field. This is crucial for learning the details. For instance, if you're in sales, don't limit yourself to the sales office. Visit the actual sales sites, study the field, and then engage in selling. With a deeper understanding of the details, your sales efforts are likely to yield better results.

CHANGES IN THE COMPANY AND A CONFLICT OF CHOICES

In 1980, Korea was experiencing turbulent times following the assassination of President Park Chung-hee and the rise of a new military government. The Korea National Oil Corporation (KNOC), where I was employed, found itself amidst these sweeping changes. During this period, affected by the second oil crisis, Gulf, which held a 50% stake in KNOC, decided to sell its entire stake in August 1980. Sensing a crisis, the government opted to privatize KNOC, placing the fate of Korea's leading public enterprise at a crossroads.

At the time, KNOC was a prestigious company, boasting annual sales of 4 trillion won and a net profit of 400 billion won. Consequently, it was expected that major corporations like Samsung and Hyundai would be interested in acquiring KNOC. However, to everyone's surprise, Sunkyung (now SK), then only a top 10 company, took over. This acquisition catapulted Sunkyung to the forefront of

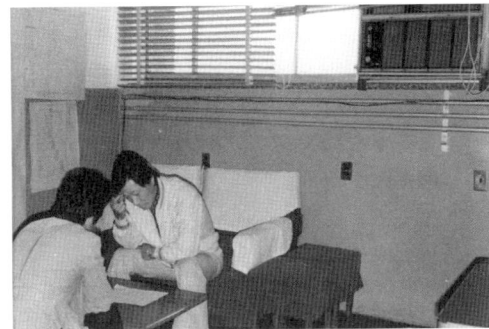
In the KNOC office

Korea's conglomerates. Being intimately familiar with the internal workings of KNOC, I watched with a heavy heart as this emblematic public enterprise was taken over by Sunkyung.

Following the acquisition, Sunkyung's executives began managing KNOC. As a director at the time, I was deeply affected by these changes. I faced a critical decision: Should I continue working under the new Sunkyung management, or should I seek a new path?

In fact, ever since joining the company, I had harbored a dream of establishing my own business and creating a stage. I had been preparing for it gradually, but the responsibility of supporting my struggling family often delayed my plans. However, the unexpected changes at the company felt like a sign from destiny, urging me to pursue my dream.

Admittedly, there were concerns. With no savings and being in

Changes in the company and conflict of choices

my mid-40s, the risks were significant. But my decision was firm; I had crossed the Rubicon, symbolizing a point of no return. Despite the lack of savings and advancing age, I was equipped with dreams and skills. I was confident that my abilities honed at KNOC would stand me in good stead in my future endeavors. My experience wasn't just theoretical; I had practical knowledge and expertise gained from fieldwork, coupled with a fiery will and belief in my capabilities.

I had been responsible for overseeing KNOC's extensive factory facilities, which spanned over 7 million square meters. This experience had not only sharpened my attention to detail but also honed my people skills and leadership abilities. These skills are often undervalued, but I understood their importance and was ready to leverage them in my new venture.

I was acutely aware that someone with my abilities could achieve

I had been responsible for overseeing KNOC's extensive factory facilities, which spanned over 7 million square meters. This experience had not only sharpened my attention to detail but also honed my people skills and leadership abilities. These skills are often undervalued, but I understood their importance and was ready to leverage them in my new venture. I was acutely aware that someone with my abilities could achieve significantly higher profits in business. Where an average person might see a 10% profit margin, I was confident that I could generate as much as a 30% profit.

significantly higher profits in business. Where an average person might see a 10% profit margin, I was confident that I could generate as much as a 30% profit. This belief stemmed from my unique skills and expertise. I was certain that these attributes would ensure my success, regardless of the circumstances. As it turned out, my confidence was well-founded, as I proved to be right in my assessment.

CHAPTER 5

FAITH AND TRUST BUILT WITH SADE

CRISIS IS THE BEST OPPORTUNITY TO BUILD FAITH

COMPETENCY CREATES FAITH IN YOUR ABILITY

People often tell me, 'You seem to have a faith in yourself that you can make anything happen.' They remark on my exceptional ability to find solutions to problems that appear impossible to them, and my knack for meeting the right people to resolve these issues. Often, I only realize the extent of my abilities after hearing others describe them. It seems I perform many of these actions almost subconsciously, as they have become second nature to me.

SADE: THE BEGINNING OF BUILDING FAITH

Reflecting on when I developed this aspect of myself that people notice, I realize I wasn't always this way. There were many occasions in my life when I, too, gave up on seemingly impossible tasks.

However, as I continued to expand my knowledge and skills, I found myself giving up less frequently. At the core of this growing expertise and confidence was my experience with SaDe.

FIRST SECRET: EXPERIENCE OF SOLVING PROBLEMS ON MY OWN

Firstly, my challenging family circumstances played a significant role in strengthening me, and the hardships I endured during my college days as a live-in tutor also honed my ability to overcome difficulties. More importantly, my military service experience and the lessons learned there significantly developed my inner resilience.

However, upon reflecting on my life, I realized that my self-belief grew stronger each time I solved a problem independently. This sense of achievement, gained without relying on others, was pivotal.

If I hadn't had the experience of climbing those stairs on my own on the ship returning from Japan at the tender age of four, or if I hadn't had the experience of climbing up the ladder to fix an electrical issue in Jeonju by myself just after college, my life might have been much like anyone else's. I might not have possessed the strength to persevere through tough situations.

Yet, I did climb those stairs onto the ship, facing potential danger. I have encountered and overcome more challenging situations with my own capabilities than many others. I believe these experiences constitute the first secret to my firm belief that I can achieve anything.

SECOND SECRET: DEVELOP SKILLS

It's remarkable to see the results when personal successes accumulate. These experiences gradually transform into skills. By focusing on the power of detail, as I emphasize here, your skills can reach an advanced level. With such proficiency, you naturally gain the confidence to tackle any problem you encounter.

However, for those who haven't developed such skill levels, challenging tasks can seem insurmountable. The Bible says, "Ask, and it will be given to you; seek, and you will find; knock, and it will be opened to you." I firmly believe that anyone can become competent by applying these principles. Often, self-deprecating thoughts like 'I can't do it because I lack skills' emerge from a recognition of one's limitations. But to truly believe in your capabilities, developing your skills is the first step.

THIRD SECRET: RISE TO CHALLENGES

To enhance your skills, you must overcome the habit of giving up and embrace challenges that come your way. If you don't take on challenges, nothing changes. Progress only happens when you rise to meet these challenges. Remember, everything you do accumulates as knowledge and experience, eventually contributing to your skill development.

FOURTH SECRET: STUDY THE DETAILS

To develop higher-level skills, you need to study details meticulously. For instance, if you are selling over the phone, you only achieve 10% of effective communication. Real learning happens when you meet people in person, observing and understanding cues from their eyes and facial expressions.

There was a time when Ilsung faced excessively high taxes. Through careful and detailed research, we identified a reasonable exemption. When we presented this to local government officials, they were astonished and inquired how we discovered these regulations. This approach enabled us to significantly reduce our tax burden.

Another time, our employees faced a challenge when they shipped products to China. The goods were held up during the airport screening process, and clearance was denied. Initially, we sent our employees to Beijing to resolve the issue, but the authorities were unresponsive.

Realizing the gravity of the situation, I decided to fly to Beijing and personally intervene, despite my limited proficiency in Chinese. My direct involvement led to a meeting with a top official in China. During our conversation, I noticed discrepancies from the account I had received from my employees. As we spoke, I sensed the potential to develop a positive rapport with the official. Discovering that we shared the same last name, Chang, served as an ice breaker. I seized the moment to present him with a gift I had brought, which he gladly accepted. Our subsequent interactions, including a shared meal and a karaoke session, warmed him to our cause and ultimately helped resolve the problem.

This experience reinforced my belief in the power of face-to-face meetings. Direct interactions allow for the reading of facial expressions and the grasping of subtle details, which are crucial for conveying truths and solving problems.

CRISIS IS A GOLDEN OPPORTUNITY TO BUILD FAITH

Everyone faces crises in life, varying in scale and impact. Life, by its nature, is a journey of ups and downs. The real challenge lies in our attitude as we navigate these highs and lows.

In times of crisis, people generally respond in one of two ways. Some become overwhelmed by the crisis, allowing fear to paralyze them, leading them to a metaphorical abyss. Others, however, perceive a crisis as a chance for growth and self-improvement, emerging stronger and more capable. The choice ultimately lies in your hands. If you respond with despair, you risk falling into the depths of the crisis. But if you approach it as an opportunity for development, you can use the experience to grow and evolve. This mindset is what can transform a crisis into a stepping stone for personal and professional growth.

I can speak about crises with confidence because my belief in my ability to overcome challenges is deeply intertwined with my experiences of crisis. Throughout my life, I've faced numerous crises, with perhaps the earliest being the time I climbed the stairs of a ship returning from Japan at the age of four. I was acutely aware of the danger, knowing a single misstep could be disastrous. Had I been overwhelmed by fear, I might have retreated into my parents' arms. Instead, I chose to face the challenge, climbing each step despite the risk. This decision not only strengthened me as a child but also instilled a belief that there was nothing I couldn't face and overcome. It was a formative experience, demonstrating the growth that comes from confronting and surviving a crisis.

Since then, I've encountered several crises in my life. Each time, I chose not to evade but to confront these challenges head-on. Naturally, this approach has continually strengthened my inner resolve.

I trace this fortitude back to overcoming that first crisis on the ship. Each successive crisis I've conquered has bolstered my belief in my capabilities. Overcoming major challenges has a way of diminishing the significance of smaller problems, imbuing me with confidence. Once you've triumphed over a significant obstacle, other issues seem less daunting, and you feel prepared to tackle them all.

Having the belief that you can accomplish something is crucial, as it fills your life with confidence and vitality. When confronted with difficult challenges, most people lose hope and succumb to despair, allowing their lives to metaphorically teeter on the edge of a cliff. However, with the conviction that you can overcome obstacles,

Since then, I've encountered several crises in my life. Each time,
I chose not to evade but to confront these challenges head-on.
I trace this fortitude back to overcoming that first crisis on the ship.
Each successive crisis I've conquered has bolstered my belief in
my capabilities.

you can rise again without falling, even in the face of adversity. I firmly believe that it is this resilience that defines a truly successful life.

A SUDDEN HEALTH CRISIS
OVERCOMING IT WITH RELIGIOUS FAITH

Since my youth, I have enjoyed sports, particularly tennis, and I have always had a passion for hiking. This active lifestyle gave me confidence in my health. During my tenure at KNOC, I maintained a rigorous routine: waking up at 6 a.m., hiking a nearby mountain for 30 to 40 minutes, and then running down to start my day with a shower, breakfast, and heading off to work. My confidence in my physical well-being was unshakable. However, in my mid-30s, while managing the long-distance oil pipeline construction project in Daegu, I was suddenly struck by an unexpected illness.

At first, I assumed it was just the flu. After visiting a doctor, I was prescribed medication and assured that I would recover soon. However, even after taking the medicine, my condition didn't improve, and I developed a fever. Then, a doctor at the general hospital suggested that drinking alcohol might help, so I tried drinking vodka straight from a beer glass. Unfortunately, this only caused my fever to spike further.

Despite my worsening condition, my work schedule from Thursday to Friday prevented me from seeking immediate medical attention. It wasn't until Saturday that I managed to visit a doctor, who happened to be a high school friend with an internal medicine clinic nearby. He was alarmed upon seeing my state and urgently referred me to a hospital. Once hospitalized, I had to fast in preparation for various tests. During my stay, it became increasingly clear to me that my condition was serious and required attention at a larger hospital. However, I hesitated to express this to my friend, fearing it might offend him. I waited, hoping he would suggest the move, but when he didn't, my patience wore thin. Eventually, overwhelmed with frustration and concern for my health, I confronted him angrily, declaring my intention to transfer to a larger hospital immediately.

When it was time for meals, I ate clear porridge and cabbage miso soup that my mother had brought. Although these were soft foods suitable for a patient, I suddenly experienced severe stomach upset. The cabbage leaves felt like they were scratching my insides, probably exacerbated by the stress from my earlier outburst at the doctor. The pain became unbearable. In haste, I caught a taxi and rushed to Daegu Dongsan Hospital.

Upon arrival, I was suffering from what appeared to be intestinal bleeding, indicated by bloody stools. I was immediately admitted to Dongsan Hospital, where the bleeding persisted. The doctors con-

My wedding photo

With my loving wife and first child

ducted various tests but were initially unable to determine the cause of my condition. They informed me that if the bleeding continued for more than ten days, intestinal surgery would be necessary. The thought of undergoing surgery and the physical impact of it saddened me deeply.

Fortunately, after an anxious ten-day wait, the bleeding ceased, and surgery was deemed unnecessary. However, my recovery was far from complete. Normally weighing 65 kg, I had lost 7 kg during my illness, leaving me looking skeletal.

While I continued my stay in the hospital, a few members from a local church visited my room to pray for me. Although I was not religious at the time, I welcomed their prayers, thinking they might be beneficial. Among the visitors was the director from the prayer center, who also came to pray for me. Intriguingly, each time someone prayed, I felt a sense of calm and a growing confidence in my recovery. The prayer center director visited me daily for nearly 15 days to offer prayers.

This act of kindness seemed to have a profound impact on my wife, who then began attending the prayer center regularly to pray and listen to sermons. After being discharged from the hospital, I joined her in visiting the prayer center, staying there to receive further prayers. Remarkably, my health improved significantly, and I was eventually declared completely cured. It was an outcome that even the hospital had not been able to achieve. This miraculous recovery deeply touched both my wife and me, leading us to embrace Christianity.

CRISIS FOLLOWING THE SUDDEN TERRORIST ATTACKS OF 9/11

For many years, I had successfully grown the company by keenly understanding both domestic and international market trends, and by making bold investments in facilities and factory expansions. My predictions consistently proved accurate, and the volume of orders matched the expanded capacity of our factories. This approach demonstrated that by creating and implementing a business plan in anticipation of market conditions, a company can grow not only by securing cost competitiveness but also by branching into new product lines.

In the late 1990s, we received information indicating a resurgence in the U.S. power plant market. Perceiving this as a significant opportunity, I focused on the American market and invested 20 billion won to construct an additional factory, spanning 60,000 square meters. As anticipated, Ilsung secured substantial plant orders from

U.S. companies.

However, in 2001, the unexpected occurred: the 9/11 terrorist attacks in the United States. This catastrophic event shocked not only the U.S. but the entire world. The attacks resulted in the tragic loss of over 3,130 lives, exceeding the 2,330 casualties of the Pearl Harbor attack by 800. The economic repercussions were immediate, with the stock market crashing and the U.S. third quarter GDP recording negative growth. Global trade diminished compared to the previous year. Subsequently, the bankruptcy of Enron, a large American corporation, further exacerbated the situation, leading to a widespread economic downturn.

Given the global impact of the 9/11 attacks, I knew that Ilsung would not remain unaffected. Indeed, not long afterward, about 50% of the plant orders we were receiving from U.S. power plants were canceled. This was an unexpected blow, especially since we had just expanded our factory in anticipation of growth in the American market. Suddenly, I found myself with an underutilized facility.

In response to this crisis, I embarked on extensive travels around the world to secure new orders, attempting to compensate for losses in the American market. However, the setback in the U.S. was so substantial that I struggled to find enough new business to cover the shortfall. Over three years, factoring in facility investment and land purchase costs, our losses amounted to a staggering 10 billion won.

Instead of succumbing to frustration or defeat, I adhered to my usual approach: when facing a loss in one area, I worked even harder in another to recover. This time was no different. I dedicated myself to exploring and developing new markets globally. I firmly believed that heaven never betrayed those who tried.

This approach paid off as we successfully entered new markets, including Venezuela. Despite the initial losses caused by the U.S. crisis, Ilsung emerged from this period with valuable experience, ultimately becoming a stronger and more resilient company.

TEARING UP THE CONTRACT WITH THE BRAZILIAN STATE-OWNED COMPANY

In 2003, we were involved in a project contracted with Petrobras, Brazil's national oil company. We had completed about 50% of the work, but there was an issue: we hadn't received any payment. Concerned about the potential for a major problem, I sent my eldest son, who is now the CEO of Ilsung Hisco, to Brazil to investigate the situation.

Upon his arrival in Brazil, my son inquired about the delayed payment. The Brazilian executive apologized and assured him that the payment would be transferred soon. Trusting this promise, my son returned home. However, despite the assurances, the payment still did not materialize. My son made a second trip to Brazil, pressing for an explanation. Once again, he was met with apologies and a renewed promise of payment. Relying on the executive's word for a second time, my son returned, but still, no payment was received.

Frustrated by the broken promises, my son resolved to prevent a recurrence of this situation. He took decisive action by drafting a new contract with a specific clause requiring immediate payment for 50% of the completed work. This was a significant change from the previous contract, which had vague terms regarding payment.

My son embarked on his third trip to Brazil with the new contract in hand. During a meeting with the Brazilian executive, he presented the original contract, questioning its validity since over 50% of the work was completed without any payment. In a bold move, he tore up the contract right in front of the executive, visibly startling him. The executive, in a panic, implored my son to reconsider, insisting they intended to keep honoring the contract. My son firmly countered, questioning the meaning of a contract when promises were not kept.

The Brazilian executive, with no excuses left, fell silent. Seizing the moment, my son presented the new contract, stipulating an immediate 50% payment, with the remaining amount to be paid in two installments of 30% and 20%. Left with no alternative, the executive signed the new contract.

Upon my son's return to Korea, the 50% payment was promptly received, marking his strategy a complete success.

However, the issue with the Brazilian company was far from resolved. As the deadline for order delivery approached, 30% of the remaining payment had not been received. Concerned that the final

20% might also be delayed, my son made another trip to Brazil. He confronted the Brazilian executive, warning that continued delays would force us to take action. Predictably, the executive promised imminent payment. My son, giving him the benefit of the doubt, returned to Korea. But, as before, the payment did not arrive.

Resorting to the strategy that had worked previously, my son prepared a new contract and flew back to Brazil. He dramatically tore up the existing contract in front of the executive. Taken aback, the executive listened as my son presented the terms of the new contract. This contract stipulated that Ilsung would only deliver the order after receiving 100% of the balance. Additionally, it included compensation for costs incurred due to the Brazilian party's broken promises, including airfare and financial losses from the delayed payment, amounting to several hundred thousand dollars, to be paid after order delivery.

Reluctantly, the Brazilian executive signed the new contract. Consequently, Ilsung received the full payment and shipped the order. The only remaining issue was the additional costs. Brazil requested a slight reduction in these costs, which we agreed to. Thanks to my son's persistent efforts, the Petrobras project, which had nearly spiraled into a fiasco, was successfully completed.

NON-PAYMENT CRISIS WITH A U.S. COMPANY
TURNING CRISIS INTO OPPORTUNITY!

In the early 2000s, Ilsung faced yet another non-payment issue, this time involving a transaction with a U.S. company. Unlike the Brazilian company, where we preemptively resolved the payment problem before delivering the order, the situation with the U.S. company became more complicated. We had already delivered the order without securing payment. At that time, one of our employees cautioned against shipping the order without receiving payment first. However, I overruled this advice, confident in the letter of credit I had signed and instructed the shipment to proceed.

My decision was influenced by a personal encounter I had with the senior manager of the American company during a business trip to the United States. We met at the Chicago airport, where he requested that we ship the order prior to payment. Normally, I insist on receiving payment before dispatching orders, but his demeanor

Ceremony Commemorating the Completion of the Industrial Bank of Ulsan - December 26, 2005

appeared so gentle and trustworthy that I decided to trust him and agreed to ship the order before receiving payment.

However, despite the passage of time after the delivery, the payment of about $2.5 million from the American company, equivalent to $25 million in today's value, had not been received. This sum was substantial enough to severely impact Ilsung if it remained unpaid. Upon investigation, I discovered that the American company was facing a crisis due to accumulated losses.

Many advised me to file a lawsuit immediately, but I was reluctant. I feared that legal action would be time-consuming and, in the interim, Ilsung could face its own crisis.

This situation was probably the worst nightmare I had experienced, bringing me close to a nervous breakdown. During this period, while flying to check a project at a hydroelectric power plant in Cambodia, I was engulfed in pessimism. The thought crossed my mind that if it were possible, I might jump out of the plane to escape

Commemoration of the Remodeling of the Ulsan Branch of Korea Development Bank - March 6, 2023

the overwhelming stress.

Regaining my composure amidst the crisis, I took decisive action to resolve the financial issues. This involved selling off two parcels of land: a 3,300 square meter plot in Hogye-dong, Buk-gu, Ulsan, previously earmarked for a new factory, and another 132,000 square meter property intended for a seaside factory.

Indeed, it's often said that crisis begets opportunity. True to this adage, shortly after navigating through these challenges, Ilsung was approached by the Korea Development Bank. Recognizing our leadership in overseas exports and our solid reputation, the bank expressed interest in investing in our technology. Consequently, Ilsung secured an investment of 15 billion won from the Korea Development Bank on the condition that the bank became a shareholder. This financial boost enabled us to construct a factory on a 60,000 square meter site we had previously acquired. Following the factory's completion, a surge in orders ensued.

The influx of orders was so substantial that within less than a year, there were complaints about the factory's limited capacity. To understand the situation better, I visited the factory early each morning for a month. The factory was indeed overcrowded due to the high volume of incoming supplies, leaving inadequate space for material storage. It was evident that this cramped condition would lead to unnecessary expenses if we had to resort to renting additional space externally.

Following these developments, I resumed my search for a suitable site to build another factory. During this process, I discovered a 73,000 square meter site adjacent to our current factory. Although it was already under contract with another party, signed a year prior, I saw the proximity of this site as a significant cost-saving opportunity and a potentially ideal expansion. Believing it to be a stroke of luck, I pursued the chance to purchase this factory, requiring a sum of 17 billion won.

To finance this acquisition, I reached out to the head of Woori Bank for support. They initially responded positively. However, complications arose when the seller of the factory site stipulated that the transaction had to be completed within 20 days, or they would withdraw their offer. This time constraint required immediate action. I promptly made inquiries at Woori Bank, learning that a board meeting would need to convene within this timeframe to authorize the payment. I escalated the matter to the bank's senior management in Seoul, urging a swift board meeting. Remarkably, within 30 minutes, I received confirmation that it was possible. The board moved quickly, and the factory site contract was signed without delay.

At that moment, I felt profoundly grateful. For a month, we had been struggling to locate a suitable factory site. It seemed to me that providence had intervened, providing us with a much-needed expansion opportunity right beside our current facility.

KIKO INCIDENT AND TURNING THE TABLES 10 YEARS LATER

Around 2009-2010, despite receiving prestigious accolades such as the Trader of the Year award and the Gold Tower Order of Industrial Service Merit, Ilsung was grappling internally with a significant financial challenge. This was the period when the 'KIKO' (Knock-In, Knock-Out) financial derivative product was prevalent. Unbeknownst to me, one of our employees had subscribed to this product.

KIKO, a derivative based on exchange rates, was designed to allow companies to sell at a predetermined exchange rate if the rates fluctuated within a specific range. Many export-oriented companies like Ilsung, which were vulnerable to exchange rate fluctuations, were attracted to KIKO, believing it could mitigate exchange rate risks. Consequently, Ilsung also subscribed to this product, following the prevailing trend.

However, I later discovered a concerning clause in the KIKO

contract. It indicated that substantial losses could be incurred if the exchange rate strayed beyond the set range. Specifically, KIKO contracts offered limited benefits to exporters only within a certain range when the exchange rate fell. If the rate dropped beyond this range, the contract was automatically terminated. On the other hand, if the exchange rate rose, exporters faced unlimited losses. This structure of KIKO posed a significant financial risk for companies like Ilsung, who had opted into this derivative without full awareness of its implications.

In 2008, the subprime mortgage crisis occurred in the United States and spread throughout the world, which caused the global financial debacle. The global financial crisis of 2008 led to a sharp increase in foreign exchange rates, which significantly impacted companies like Ilsung that had subscribed to KIKO, a high-risk foreign exchange derivative product. The problem began when we didn't thoroughly scrutinize the terms of the KIKO contract upon signing up for it.

As a result of this oversight, Ilsung experienced substantial losses. Between 2007 and 2008, we signed KIKO contracts worth $211.5 million to hedge against exchange rate fluctuations. However, the rapidly rising exchange rates soon after signing the contract led to a loss of approximately 100 billion won by 2011. The situation was exacerbated by accruing interest, which added a substantial amount to our losses.

Additionally, the global economic downturn significantly affected the industrial sector, forcing companies, including Ilsung, to accept low-priced orders from domestic clients. This led to a further decrease in our external credibility, hampering our ability to secure overseas orders and causing a liquidity crisis. In an attempt to navigate through this crisis, I sought investment funds, but it was not enough to stem the tide of financial challenges. Consequently, in 2012, Ilsung declared bankruptcy and entered court receivership for corporate rehabilitation. Control of the company was eventually transferred to Yonhap Asset Management (UAMCO) as part of the rehabilitation process.

At that time, the global financial crisis was a challenge for all companies, but Ilsung was thriving. We were achieving $200 million in exports, had received the Gold Tower Order of Industrial Service Merit, and were anticipating sales of 1 trillion won. Had we steered clear of the KIKO product, the sharp rise in exchange rates could have yielded substantial profits. Unfortunately, the KIKO incident dashed these aspirations.

The situation was particularly disheartening as it occurred during a period when Ilsung and I were contributing significantly to Korea's exports, as evidenced by the awarding of the Gold Tower Order of Industrial Service Merit. This made the impact of the KIKO incident all the more tragic. I regretted that a bit more caution and prudence on my part could have prevented this outcome.

Ilsung was not the only company affected by KIKO. Among the

700 small and medium-sized enterprises that subscribed to KIKO, most suffered significant losses and many went bankrupt. The total damage was estimated at 3.2 trillion won, a sum with a serious impact on the national economy. In response, I joined forces with other affected companies to form the KIKO Joint Countermeasures Committee. This coalition actively pursued legal action and achieved its first victory in a civil lawsuit in 2012. Finally, in 2019, eleven years after the KIKO incident, the Financial Supervisory Service held the banks accountable. A financial dispute mediation decision was reached, ordering the payment of 25.5 billion won to the four affected companies, including Ilsung.

After entering court receivership in 2012, Ilsung faced a challenging period. However, the company managed to recover its previous performance levels and achieved a financial surplus for the first time in a decade by 2020. By the end of 2021, Ilsung had repaid the investment from UAMCO and regained its management rights.

Despite experiencing the most severe crisis since its inception, Ilsung continued to secure significant contracts. In April 2013, we signed a $10 million contract with UOP in the U.S., followed by a $5 million supply contract with SHELL, a global oil company, for supplies to the U.S. and Canada. Moreover, Ilsung was honored to be the only Korean company selected as a long-term preferred supplier under the Enterprise Framework Agreement (EFA) with Shell. This selection placed us among the top five plant manufacturers worldwide linked to Shell.

Ilsung's sales figures continued to rise steadily. In 2020, our sales reached 49.5 billion won, marking a 61% increase from the previous year, and we reported an operating profit of 3.3 billion won, culminating in a surplus. This turnaround not only demonstrated the resilience of Ilsung but also testified to the company's hidden strength amidst adversity.

MY FIRST EXPERIENCE OF JAIL
SPECIAL TRAINING IN SELF-REFLECTION

The repercussions of the KIKO incident extended beyond Ilsung's bankruptcy and had a profound personal impact on me, culminating in a jail sentence. During this tumultuous period, I was actively seeking investors to provide a much-needed lifeline for the company. My efforts led me to financial institutions like IBK Capital, and I was successful in securing an investment of 50 billion won.

The financial companies involved undertook a comprehensive evaluation of Ilsung's potential for a future rebound. They considered our financial structure and past export performance in their assessment. Additionally, investment feasibility reports played a crucial role in securing this significant investment. These reports highlighted Ilsung's increasing sales in global markets and its robust technological capabilities. Based on these favorable evaluations, the investment proposal was approved by the boards of these financial companies.

The review of Ilsung's investments by the financial companies began in June 2010. However, the process was delayed, and the investment funds were not received until over a year later in 2011. But Ilsung had continued to lose money due to the KIKO contracts, making it challenging to stave off bankruptcy, even with the incoming investment. Had this investment arrived in 2010, it might

Entering prison in my late 70s was something I had never envisioned. Facing this unexpected turn in my life, I resolved to use my time in prison for special training in self-reflection. I shared with them confidently that my time in prison was a period of special training. I assured them that I was stronger than before and ready to collaborate for a better future.

have made a difference. Ultimately, despite the investment, Ilsung declared bankruptcy.

The aftermath posed a problem for the executives of the financial companies who had decided to invest in Ilsung. I believe there was a provision in the Financial Services Act penalizing those who invested in a company that went bankrupt within a year of the investment. Consequently, these executives, upon reviewing the financial statements and investment feasibility reports, accused me of accounting fraud and filed a lawsuit.

Subsequently, I was indicted, tried, and sentenced to four years in prison. I felt the ruling was unfair and filed an appeal, but the court upheld the original decision.

Entering prison in my late 70s was something I had never envisioned. Facing this unexpected turn in my life, I resolved to use my time in prison for special training in self-reflection. It became an opportunity for me to contemplate my actions and to retrain myself. Upon my arrival in prison, I noticed that the guards treated me with a degree of respect, acknowledging my educational background as a graduate of Seoul National University.

There was a prison guard who treated me particularly well. Whenever I had a visitor, this guard always escorted me to see them. He would also give me books to read and encouraged me to inform him of any difficulties I faced. With his help, I was able to solve various problems, which made my time in jail much more bearable. My eldest son also did everything he could to secure my early release, including filing a special pardon petition. Eventually, I was released on parole after 3 years and 2 months.

After my release, I visited the United States to meet with my business partners. People from all around congratulated me on my release and even presented me with bouquets of flowers. Their pats on the back and reassurances that I could always start over again moved me deeply. These were the people who had been with me during my most successful and shining moments. Even when I was in prison, they flew in from America to visit me twice. Normally, when a businessman faces bankruptcy and imprisonment, their business partners turn away from them. However, in my case, they remained loyal under all circumstances. Their unwavering support made me confident that with people like them by my side, I could certainly rise again. I shared with them confidently that my time in prison was a period of special training. I assured them that I was stronger than before and ready to collaborate for a better future.

THE SECRET TO UNION-FREE MANAGEMENT
TRUST RELATIONSHIPS WITH EMPLOYEES

In the past, there was a question that often arose during media interviews: How was it possible for Ilsung to operate a union-free business? Some speculated that the chairman was coercively managing the company, preventing the formation of unions. However, I never once opposed the formation of a union and had no intention of interfering. On the contrary, I saw the value in promoting constructive union activities. I even suggested establishing a union several times, believing that a constructive approach could aid the company's development.

This is not to say that there were no attempts to establish a union at Ilsung. When the trend of forming labor unions swept through Korea, I heard rumors about a similar movement within our company. Honestly, this news bewildered me; I believed that I had forged strong bonds with the employees and that our communication was effective. The idea of them wanting to create a labor union left me internally uncomfortable. Yet, I couldn't forbid them from forming a union. Recognizing that nearly every company had a labor union, I signaled my approval of their initiative. I also acknowledged that establishing a labor union could positively impact the protection of employee rights.

One day, amidst my usual work, an employee approached me. He expressed deep regret, saying he could no longer stay with the company. When I inquired about his reasons, he hesitated, indicating he couldn't disclose them. Respecting his privacy and possible undisclosed reasons, I accepted his resignation.

However, I later discovered that the employee had misrepresented his identity to join our company with the specific intention of establishing a labor union at Ilsung. There was a period when labor activists, masquerading as job seekers, infiltrated companies to engage in labor movements, including union formation. The resignation of this particular employee also happened when such activities were prevalent. The employee in question was tasked with forming a union at Ilsung. He got hired, rallied several employees, met the requirements for establishing a union, and actively pushed for its creation. However, establishing a union required the consent of other employees, and he encountered significant opposition.

One employee who opposed the union said, "When my baby was ill and I couldn't afford the surgery, my boss discreetly covered the hospital expenses, enabling the surgery to go ahead. Approving the union would feel like a betrayal to my boss." Another employee added, "I am also against it. When I was getting married and searching for a house, the boss stepped in and helped me find a comfortable home. I can't betray him." Many employees expressed similar sentiments, opposing the plan, and the labor activist failed to secure any supporting votes. Eventually, he abandoned the attempt to establish a union, resigned, and left the company, as his true intention was never genuinely to work for us.

These are some of the untold stories behind Ilsung's non-union management. Since those events, no union has been formed at Ilsung. I believe this enduring trust-based relationship with our employees was also fostered by my adherence to the principles of SaDe.

COMMUNICATION AND SHARING: KEYS TO TRUST!

I think the reason Ilsung employees opposed the establishment of a union is because they shared a trusting relationship with me. My approach to thinking about and caring for my employees is fully reflected in Ilsung's company motto. Let's revisit it:

'Ensure a prosperous life for those who work.'
'Find and take responsibility for your own work.'
'Operate democratically and autonomously.'

Who do you think is at the heart of this company motto? I crafted it step by step, always considering the employees' perspective. This is because I believe that the success of my employees directly contributes to my own and the company's success. Thus, I constantly thought about ways to help my employees flourish. To this end,

Hiking excursion with employees

I made sure to cater to their needs. For instance, Ilsung employees enjoy a group hiking excursion at least once a month, followed by a company dinner. This event is just one part of our broader approach.

In 1989, we offered all our employees an opportunity to travel abroad. I initiated this event because, as an export-driven company, Ilsung needed to embrace foreign trends to boost employee morale. At that time, overseas travel was uncommon and costly. Nonetheless, the company sponsored a trip to Taiwan for all 20 employees. Conveniently, Taehwa Tour company was located nearby, allowing us to secure a tour guide through them. The entire team landed in Taipei, Taiwan's capital, toured the city, and then visited the port cities of Hualien and Hualien, exploring various tourist attractions. I fondly remember a trip to a village in the alpine region where we all participated in gymnastics and danced joyfully.

2009 company workshop

I believe that the absence of a labor union at Ilsung is due to the strong relationship between the boss and the employees, grounded in mutual trust. Trust is not built overnight. It accumulates gradually through shared experiences, like looking into each other's eyes, eating together, sharing concerns, and traveling together. The essence of this trust must be mutual, not one-sided. If you extend trust and sincerity first, the other person is likely to reciprocate that trust.

I am grateful to have developed a knack for creating trusting relationships, perhaps more so than anyone else. My approach to relationships isn't based on specific plans; it's about instinctively knowing how to treat others from the moment I meet them. I trust my intuition in interactions, and before I realize it, a trusting relationship has often formed. When I visited the United States after

Ganwoljae, Ulju-gun: 2022 Ulsan Fall Hiking Event

my release from prison, people congratulated and encouraged me instead of shunning me. I believe this was possible because of the trusting relationships we had developed.

I believe that communication and sharing are the two most crucial elements in creating a trusting relationship. Firstly, there must be an effort to communicate. This involves meeting and talking frequently. To facilitate this, a conducive environment is necessary, and sometimes, gifts can play a role. Alongside communication, there must be sharing. Here, sharing refers to recognizing what the other person needs and fulfilling that need. Such sharing should be genuine. When communication and sharing are practiced sincerely, a relationship of trust will naturally evolve.

WHY THE INDUSTRIAL PEACE AWARD MATTERS MORE TO ME THAN THE GOLD TOWER ORDER OF INDUSTRIAL SERVICE MERIT

When I received the Gold Tower Order of Industrial Service Merit, people were understandably impressed, as it's awarded to those who have made significant contributions to the country. This honor is especially significant as it recognizes outstanding contributions to the development of the national industry. The fact that President Lee Myung-bak personally presented it to me during the 47th Trade Day ceremony at COEX in Samseong-dong, Seoul, underscores its prestige.

However, the accolade I hold in the highest regard is not the Gold Tower Order of Industrial Service Merit. While it is undoubtedly the most prestigious award I have received, what one values most can vary based on personal experiences. You might find it odd, but the award I cherish the most is the Gyeongnam Industrial Peace Award, of which I was the inaugural recipient. Some might question

I received the 1st Gyeongnam Industrial Peace Award on June 29, 1991.

how I can compare a regional award to national honors, but my perspective is different. The Gyeongnam Industrial Peace Award holds a special significance for me personally.

Gyeongnam, or South Gyeongsang Province, is likely home to the largest number of companies in Korea. In the past, Ulsan was not yet a metropolitan city; it was simply a city within South Gyeongsang Province. In this context, the Gyeongnam Industrial Peace Award recognized companies with exemplary management and outstanding labor-management relations among the numerous businesses in the province, including Korea's leading conglomerates. This is why I hold this award in such high esteem. Unlike most awards that focus solely on a company's performance, this one was valued for acknowledging not only the company's achievements but also the democratic nature of its labor-management culture.

At that time, there was a grand prize for the first-place winner, as well as gold, silver, bronze, iron, and stone awards. A total of 30 awards were presented to distinguished business leaders. Among all these companies, Ilsung was selected as the grand prize winner. This was particularly thrilling for my employees and me, as Ilsung had only been established just a few years earlier. It was also a significant moment for me personally, confirming my confidence in and the potential of my business endeavors. The awards ceremony was held at the KBS broadcasting station in Changwon, attracting a large audience and numerous reporters. I distinctly remember that actress Ko Hyun-jung hosted the event, adding a special touch to the occasion.

Another award that holds great meaning for me is the appreciation plaque given by our employees in 2021. Perhaps this plaque was presented as a gesture of comfort for the challenges I have faced throughout my time at Ilsung, or maybe it was to encourage me to persevere and continue striving for the company. Reflecting on this plaque brings back a flood of memories and a mix of emotions. This plaque is incredibly precious to me, as it is a testament to the heartfelt appreciation and dedication of my employees.

CHAPTER 6

SADE FOR HEALTH AND LIFE-LONG LEARNING

HEALTH IS ALSO A COMPETENCY

TWO-HOUR BAREFOOT WALK ALONG A MOUNTAIN TRAIL DESPITE BEING IN MY 80S

Even in my 80s, I maintain a routine of exercising for an hour or two every morning. These days, my preferred spot is Ulsan Grand Park, conveniently located near my house. This world-class theme park spans 3.69 square kilometers and includes a mountain, which forms part of my exercise course. With several paths to choose from, selecting my route is always an enjoyable part of my routine.

Once, I invited a younger friend from Seoul to join me for exercise. He was quite surprised to see me arrive at Ulsan Grand Park barefoot. I have been practicing barefoot walking for a long time, inspired by a book that touted its health benefits. The principle behind barefoot walking, or earthing, is that direct contact between the bare feet and the ground allows the body to absorb the earth's energy. This energy is believed to positively affect the feet, often referred to as the 'second heart,' and provide an acupressure effect. This not only strengthens the heart but is also thought to improve the health of other organs by activating various systems within the body.

There is a range of research data supporting the health benefits of earthing. One study examined the effects of earthing on blood composition, revealing a significant reduction in clumped red blood cells post-earthing. Another study found that earthing improved electrical conductivity and restored the body's natural defense system. Some even claim complete cancer remission through earthing. Clearly, earthing has substantial health benefits, and I consider myself living proof of its effects. Having practiced earthing for many years, I am more active and healthier than many younger individuals, despite being well into my 80s.

I surprised my young friend during our outing again by walking barefoot along the mountain trail for two hours. The course, mostly consisting of soft dirt, also included challenging sections with rocks and pebbles. My friend was concerned that I might hurt myself walking barefoot on such a path for two hours, but he was unaware of my experience. Initially, I could only walk on soft dirt roads. However, constantly taking off and putting on my shoes to navigate different terrain disrupted my exercise rhythm. To address this, I researched ways to walk safely on paths scattered with rock fragments. Having mastered this technique, I can now traverse even the rockiest roads without injury.

First-time observers often express concern, but I am able to hike barefoot for extended periods without any issues. The benefits of such hikes are undeniable; my body feels rejuvenated and my mind clearer. In my view, there is no better way to manage one's health.

There was a time when it rained heavily during my barefoot walk. As the rain formed puddles along the trail, most people abandoned their exercise routines and left. However, I donned a raincoat and continued walking barefoot. The sensation of stepping on water-soaked soil was uniquely refreshing—a feeling I would have missed had I given up due to the rain. Your mindset is crucial when exercising. If you tell yourself, "I cannot do this," then it becomes an insurmountable task. But if you commit to a routine and persist, it becomes an integral part of your life and significantly enhances your health.

I believe health is a form of competency. It implies that a healthy person is capable, whereas an unhealthy person is less so. Recognizing health as a competency allows you to improve it through SaDe. I have dedicated myself to enhancing both my health and competency through SaDe into my twilight years. In studying various aspects of health, I learned about the benefits of walking barefoot and taking cold baths, among other exercises. These practices have kept me healthy and capable even at my advanced age.

A COLD BATH IN THE MOUNTAINS IN THE MIDDLE OF WINTER

In addition to barefoot hiking, I have developed a fondness for taking cold baths in the winter. This practice began through my hiking experiences. I used to go hiking every Saturday, often visiting Cheonseongsan Mountain in the Yeongnam Alps. One winter, while hiking with a few employees, we came across a stream where several people were taking cold baths. Intrigued, I decided to join them, and I quickly developed a liking for it, a practice I continue to this day.

When I lived in Daegu, there was a tall mountain named Apsan, standing over 1,000 meters tall. About a 20-minute walk up the mountain there is a valley where one can take a cold bath. People venturing this far usually intend to take a cold bath. Initially, many are hesitant to plunge into the cold water due to a lack of courage.

However, I would briskly undress, dive into the cold water for my bath, and then emerge to dry off with a towel before descending the mountain. I always found it fascinating to see steam rising from my body, a result of not wiping off all the moisture. By the time I reached home, the water had dried, and the steam had disappeared.

You might wonder how one can manage to take a cold bath in the middle of winter, particularly in a mountain valley. Initially, it may seem daunting, but once you adapt, there's nothing more invigorating. Cold water baths are known for their health benefits, including reducing the spread of acute inflammatory substances, which can result from exercise. This occurs as the cold water constricts blood vessels in peripheral tissues like muscles. Most importantly, cold water baths are beneficial for boosting immunity, so I make it a point to take them in winter whenever possible.

My history with cold bathing dates back to my school years. I recall hearing about the benefits of cold water baths and finding the idea compelling. I began by using a towel soaked in cold water and rubbing it against my skin. During my time in the military, cold showers were the norm due to the absence of hot water. In the middle of winter, during field training, I often had to stay in a tent and endure the cold. This experience likely built my tolerance of cold, enabling me to embrace the challenge of winter cold baths without much difficulty.

HEALTH STRENGTHENED THROUGH EXERCISE

I have always enjoyed hiking, so I frequently climbed mountains as part of my morning exercise routine, even during my tenure at KNOC. After starting my business, my visits to the mountains continued. I would go hiking on weekends, sometimes with my employees and other times alone if no one was available to join me. Of all the mountains I have hiked, Namsan Mountain in Gyeongju remains the most memorable. This mountain is renowned for its diverse range of hiking trails, boasting as many as 63 official paths. However, I believe if you include the lesser-known, unofficial trails, the total number would exceed 100. This abundance of routes is why I frequently visited Namsan Mountain, often bringing my employees along.

One of Namsan's notable features is a restaurant named Nokjeongsa, situated at the mountain's summit. Renowned for its capacity to serve hundreds of visitors simultaneously, it is a place I remember fondly. There, I particularly enjoyed the bibimbap mixed with wild herbs. The unique taste of bibimbap enjoyed after a hike to the mountain's peak is something one must experience personally to truly appreciate.

I have always had a passion for various sports and actively engaged in those I enjoyed, such as tennis, badminton, golf, swimming, and skiing. Tennis was the first sport I took up, starting a year after I joined KNOC. I played it avidly throughout my business career. My enthusiasm for tennis was so strong that I served as the president of the Ulsan Area Tennis Association for over 10 years, beginning in 2000. During my tenure as president, my responsibilities extended beyond tennis. I also engaged in side campaigns, such as fundraising for the Tennis Association's development, providing scholarships, and assisting underprivileged students. I always valued these activities, but it was through this role that I gained a deeper appreciation for the broader purpose of a company's existence.

I took up badminton later in life, in my late 70s, considering it a sport suitable for older age due to its less demanding nature compared to tennis. Tennis can be strenuous, with the weight of the racket and ball requiring significant, instantaneous muscle strength, often straining the hands, wrists, and joints. In contrast, badminton, with its lighter racket and shuttlecock, is less taxing on the body. This makes it an ideal sport for older individuals, as it can be enjoyed without exerting excessive strain.

I am truly grateful that, even in my 80s, I can still enjoy sports such as hiking, tennis, badminton, skiing, and golf. I'm equally thankful for the good health I've maintained through these activities. Echoing the saying, "If you lose money and fame, you lose a little, but if you lose your health, you lose everything," I firmly believe that maintaining one's health is a fundamental duty of being human. Therefore, I will continue to indulge in these sports and exercises to preserve my health for as long as I can, until the day I am called to heaven.

TOP GOLF SKILLS
MY FIRST HOLE-IN-ONE

There is one particular day that I remember vividly, down to the year, month, day, and even the time: December 31, 2005, at 8:30 AM. This date is etched in my memory for a special reason: it was the day I hit my first hole-in-one at Ulsan Country Club.

As a sports enthusiast, I was already proficient in golf. I had achieved an eagle (scoring 2 under par on a single hole) perhaps four times. To commemorate these achievements, I even planted trees at the spots where I scored each eagle. However, a hole-in-one had always eluded me. It was a dream of mine to achieve this feat. In fact, a hole-in-one is such a challenging feat to accomplish that many golfers, even after playing their entire lives, may still wonder if they'll ever experience it just once.

One of the holes that day was a 150-meter par 3. The weather was cloudy and foggy, significantly reducing visibility. Moreover, there

A keepsake photo from my hole-in-one

was a bunker right in front of the green, posing a risk of dropping the ball into it with any miscalculation. In such cases, it's crucial to place the tee shot close to the green to avoid the bunker, or ideally, beyond it onto the green. I opted for the latter strategy. To achieve this, I needed to hit the ball at least 150 meters – a challenging distance, especially as I was approaching my late 60s. Nevertheless, motivated by a wager, I gathered my focus and executed a 5-iron shot. The ball soared over the fairway in a beautiful arc, easily clearing the bunker and landing on the green. However, upon reaching the green, I couldn't find the ball. I searched around, not even considering a hole-in-one as a possibility. But the ball was nowhere in sight. Then, someone shouted, "It's a hole-in-one!" I was in disbelief. Upon checking the hole, I found my ball there. It was a hole-in-one – the very achievement I had long dreamed of. The excitement was overwhelming; I wanted to jump for joy. It felt surreal, like a dream unfolding before my eyes.

There was a belief among golfers that hitting a hole-in-one would bring three years of good luck. Indeed, following my hole-in-one, I felt my fortune improving. Starting in 2006, my business experienced significant growth with an influx of orders and additional factories being constructed. Reflecting on that period still brings me immense happiness.

LEARNING TO SKI AND QUICKLY BECOMING A SKIING ENTHUSIAST

I took up skiing at the age of 59, sparked by an amusing motivation. While dining with some college friends in Seoul, the topic of skiing arose. I felt a twinge of envy, being the only one in the group who had never skied. Unbeknownst to me, a strong desire to ski ignited within me. As someone who acts swiftly upon decision-making, I found myself at Hyundai Department Store in Apgujeong-dong the very next day, purchasing a full set of ski equipment.

Even though I had never skied before, I loaded my new gear into the car and headed to the nearby Cheonmasan ski resort. Upon arrival, I saw young people practicing skiing on the beginner slope. I thought I would give it a try, but I quickly found that even the slightest movement caused me to lose balance and fall. Realizing I couldn't do it alone, I rushed to the resort office and requested a ski coach.

To my surprise, the coach took me up the hill instead of starting on the gentle slopes. As I started downhill, the coach was alongside me, but his presence wasn't much help in preventing falls. Descending the slope, I was gripped by fear, my body drenched in cold sweat. While some might consider giving up in such a scenario, for me, it only fueled my determination to master skiing.

The next time, on a Friday, I took my second son to Yongpyong Ski Resort. Considering his proficiency in skiing, I thought he could assist me as a coach. He provided detailed explanations, but, unfortunately, they didn't translate into practical help for me. It was around February 20th, close to the end of the ski season. By March 13th, the snow usually melts, making skiing impossible. This urgency made me anxious, as I was keen to learn skiing before the resort closed for the season.

I had a friend at S Oil who was an experienced skier with 22 years under his belt. This time, I sought his assistance, and he ambitiously took me to the highest slope, promising to teach me. However, we found the area unexpectedly closed. It turned out to be off-limits due to training sessions for the national team. Disappointed, we had to turn back. With only a week left in the season, my mind raced with thoughts about how to make the most of the remaining time.

Back in Ulsan, the thought consumed me that if I didn't learn to ski now, I would have to wait another year. Determined, I went to the ski resort alone on March 3rd. I noticed the weather was

Me Enjoying Skiing

warming and the snow was beginning to melt. However, I reasoned that slightly melted snow might be softer and safer for skiing. With newfound courage, I climbed up to a higher point and began to ski down. As I descended a few dozen meters, my confidence grew, almost without my realizing it. Reaching the bottom without a single fall filled me with an indescribable thrill. That day, I skied down the slope ten times, each descent bringing a wave of joy as I realized I had finally conquered skiing. From that point on, I became such an enthusiast that I went skiing every winter.

THE SECRET TO SADE LIES IN CONSTANT STUDY!

I am an avid reader, though my busy work schedule often limits my reading time. Nevertheless, I seize every opportunity to read, whether I'm traveling or getting ready for bed. Over the 30 years since starting my business, I have traveled extensively by airplane, cumulatively enough to circle the world 140 times. I also frequently traveled back and forth between Seoul. This resulted in a significant amount of time spent in transit, and I was determined not to let this time go to waste. Consequently, I began reading during these journeys, fostering a habit of always having a book at hand. You never know when you might be on the move again, and it's crucial to be prepared with a book.

Since my youth, I have indulged in reading whenever possible, enjoying books both in transit and in bed. While some may find reading while lying down uncomfortable, for me, it has always been a pleasure. The benefit of reading in this position is that you can effortlessly drift off to sleep. Waking up the next morning, I often find that the contents of the book I read the night before are vividly imprinted in my memory, making the experience even more enriching.

The most recent book I read was "The Humanities of Wealth." Initially, I thought it was a book about wealth creation, which piqued my interest. A section on George Soros, renowned as a world-class financier and investor, had a particular impact on me. It was intriguing to learn that his decision to become an investor was driven by a desire to study philosophy. This led me to ponder the connection between economics and philosophy. As I read on, I found that many prominent figures emphasized the importance of incorporating philosophy into their financial endeavors. This resonated with me and prompted me to reconsider my own philosophical beliefs.

Not long ago, I also purchased a book in its original German edition from Amazon. I discovered that a book I was interested in was not available in Korea but was in German. Having studied German as a second language in high school and continuing my studies into my second year of college, where I excelled in the subject, I felt confident in tackling the German text. In fact, German was always easier for me than English. However, upon receiving the book, I realized that it had been so long since I last read German that I had forgotten many words. Consequently, I had to read the book with the aid of a German dictionary. While this approach was time-consuming, it proved to be a fulfilling experience, allowing me to

You could say that the secret to my SaDe comes from constant study, as it's only through studying that one can grasp details. My habit of always carrying books stems from a belief in the importance of continual learning. Through this process, my SaDe is gradually shaped and expanded, often without my direct awareness. Therefore, developing the habit of consistently engaging with books is crucial.

access the information I sought.

Once, driven by my passion for reading, I purchased an extensive collection of over 50 volumes on humanities by authors from around the world. However, my busy work schedule initially prevented me from reading the entire series. A few years ago, I began to delve into these books, exploring everything from classical philosophy to the works of Hegel, Dante, and Dostoevsky. Similarly, while working at KNOC headquarters, I acquired the English edition of Encyclopedia Britannica. Time constraints meant it remained on my bookshelf, unread, until about three or four years ago, when I started to explore its contents. This reading journey has given me the sense that my inner world, which had become somewhat barren due to corporate life, was being enriched.

In truth, during the busiest periods of my work, I focused primarily on reading materials related to the company. However, in the realm of reading, it's vital to delve into a wide range of subjects rather than limiting oneself. Only by doing so can one gain an understanding of the broader world, instead of remaining confined to a narrow perspective. Thus, even today, I continue to read a variety of books.

You could say that the secret to my SaDe comes from constant study, as it's only through studying that one can grasp details. My habit of always carrying books stems from a belief in the importance of continual learning. Through this process, my SaDe is gradually shaped and expanded, often without my direct awareness. Therefore, developing the habit of consistently engaging with books is crucial.

A PASSION FOR LEARNING, EVEN IN OLD AGE!

I have always emphasized the importance of attention to detail in growing Ilsung into a globally recognized company. This focus on details, I believe, ultimately stems from studying, as it is through study that one uncovers and understands nuances. My success as a radar instructor in the military can be attributed to my dedication to studying. Similarly, my effective tenure at KNOC was a result of studying more diligently than others. During that time, I passionately read books, including those in their original languages. This habit of study extended to my work in the field, where I began to delve into the machinery I was using. It was through this deep learning that I gained intricate knowledge of the machines, achieving a level of technological expertise that garnered global recognition.

The significance of studying cannot be overstated. The concept of "lifelong study" wasn't coined without reason. While I previously discussed maintaining good health as a key purpose of human existence, studying, in fact, holds even greater importance. It is through continuous learning that one grows and ultimately leads a life befitting a mature human being. Hence, even at my advanced age, my passion for learning remains undiminished, and I continue to study earnestly.

In Shanghai, Jiaotong University is renowned as the alma mater of Jiang Zemin, the former general secretary of the Chinese Communist Party (CCP). In my mid-60s, I had the opportunity to visit China and learned about the MBA program at Jiaotong University. As a graduate of an engineering college, I had always harbored the desire to pursue an MBA. Therefore, I enrolled at this university. Some might question why I chose to study at a Chinese university, but at the time, with China's burgeoning development, I saw great potential in this decision.

The program required attendance every two weeks, so initially, I anticipated a manageable commitment. I would fly from Busan to Shanghai on Friday, attend classes on Saturday and Sunday, and return to Korea on Sunday evening. Although I had studied Chinese in preparation, upon arrival, I struggled to understand the fast-paced speech of native Chinese speakers. This led to mounting stress. Conversing with classmates and responding to professors' invitations to dine out, which they extended in amazement of my commute between Korea and China, became challenging tasks. Moreover, the

I enrolled in a program offered at Jiaotong University in Shanghai, China.

I enrolled in the Techno CEO course at the University of Ulsan Graduate School of Industrial Technology and graduated as part of its 11th class on July 18, 2022.

program involved a significant number of assignments.

During this time, thoughts of quitting began to surface. However, the president of the alumni association, deeply moved by my commitment, personally encouraged me. He remarked on the extraordinary nature of my effort, noting that the cost of my flights from Korea to China far exceeded the tuition fees. This interaction, coupled with my pride as a Korean, spurred me to persevere. Ultimately, I continued until graduation and was unexpectedly honored with the Inspiration Award at the ceremony. Initially, I thought the award was a recognition of the effort I had invested in commuting, but I was then asked to give a speech. Despite my limited Chinese, I prepared a speech, delivered it from the podium, and found myself emotionally overwhelmed by memories of the challenges I had faced.

In March 2022, at the age of 84, I completed and graduated from the Techno CEO Course at the Graduate School of Industrial Science at the University of Ulsan. I am profoundly grateful for the opportunity to engage in such learning experiences in my eighties. The reason I pursued this course was due to a recommendation from a friend and former colleague at KNOC. Despite being over 80, I enrolled without hesitation. The course, held weekly on Mondays from 7 PM to 9 PM, proved to be immensely valuable. Consequently, I encouraged my eldest son, the current CEO of Ilsung Hisco, to enroll as well. This experience reaffirmed my belief that learning should be a lifelong pursuit, regardless of age.

Furthermore, my quest for continuous learning led me to complete the international management research course at Tsinghua University in China in 2010, as part of its inaugural class, and I also studied in the AMP course of the Federation of Korean Industries. My commitment to education was recognized with an honorary doctorate from Lincoln University in the United States and a

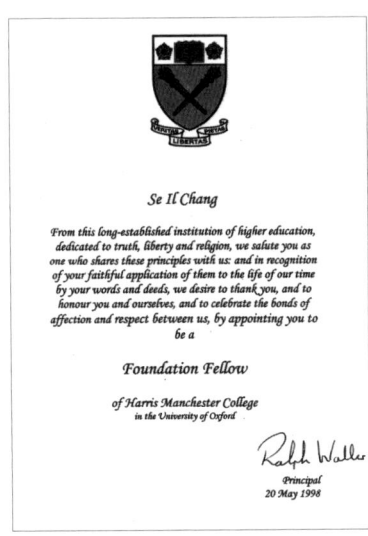
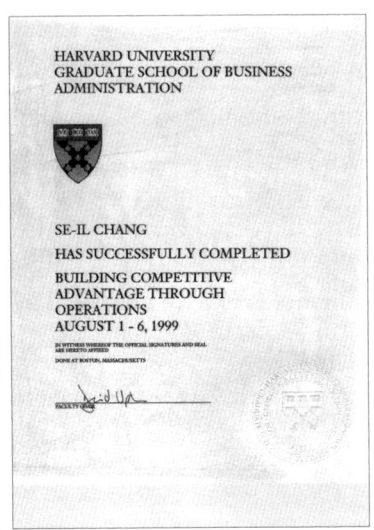

I completed the Advanced Leadership Program at Oxford University in 1997.

I completed the Building Competitive Advantage Through Operations course at Harvard University in 1999.

Foundation Fellowship from the University of Oxford in the United Kingdom.

DREAMING OF CORPORATE SOCIAL CONTRIBUTION AND MISSIONARY WORK

Initially, my focus was not on this aspect, but gradually, I began to ponder the true essence of a company. This introspection began as Ilsung grew and we started receiving requests to engage in various social activities. Reflecting on my journey, I realized I had been more involved in social activities than I had previously acknowledged, undertaking numerous initiatives that were perceived as benevolent by others.

On the business front, I have served as the chairman of the Ulsan Trading Chamber since 2000 and have also been a director of the International Management Institute since the company became a member of the Federation of Korean Industries. Socially, I have been a national representative of the Korean Red Cross since 1998 and a director of the SNU alumni association, Gwanak Club. While serving as director, I donated 100 million won to the SNU Alumni

Association for scholarships. In 2012, I also donated 100 million won each to the scholarship funds of the Gyeongbuk Middle and High School Alumni Association. In addition, I was asked by the Ministry of Justice to work for the Ulsan-Yangsan Regional Council of the Crime Prevention Committee. Also, as I mentioned before, I served as president of the Ulsan Area Tennis Association for about 10 years. During this time, I worked on various projects, such as raising funds for the Tennis Association's development, providing scholarships, and helping underprivileged students. When working for this association, I donated about 500 million won. Additionally, I worked hard to fulfill the company's social responsibilities while working as director of the suicide prevention hotline and the national arts festival for the disabled.

Generally, there is nothing more shameful than a person talking about his good deeds with his own mouth. However, there is a reason for releasing these records here: these social activities that I engage in outside of company work have given me an opportunity to think more about the reason for the existence of a company. At first, I felt like I had to deal with things like this just as a businessman. However, my view of business changed completely after I faced difficulties myself, embraced spirituality, and reflected on the social role of companies.

The first thing a company needs to do is generate profit, and once this has been achieved, its purpose should then shift to using those profits for the benefit of society, especially for those in need. This role is typically assigned to corporations rather than individuals because they are the only social organizations capable of continuously generating profits.

Think about it: no matter how much you help those in need, would it only be meaningful if it lasted? For this reason, companies are given this task. After developing this view of business, I had many dreams. As a Christian, my dream was to engage in missionary work and establish an association to support those with mental health challenges. To aid those in need, I submitted a business plan to the city. It proposed that if the city provided land, I would build a home for children from broken families. The plan also included the idea that expanding this initiative would greatly benefit society. However, the city responded that it was difficult, which saddened me.

These dreams later encountered obstacles when Ilsung faced challenges due to the KIKO incident. However, I believe that one day this problem will be resolved and Ilsung will stand tall again. I am firmly convinced that a time will come when I can realize these dreams and significantly contribute to society.

LITTLE MEMORIES OF LIFE

CRAVING GARLIC ON A BUSINESS TRIP ABROAD

While working for KNOC, I went on a business trip to America. I stayed in Houston for about a week, and by the end of the week, I had run out of kimchi. From that moment on, I started craving garlic. Koreans often can't live without garlic, and now that I couldn't have it, I felt like I was losing energy and even feeling dizzy. Then, I went to a Chinese restaurant and a Chinese old man with gray hair came out to wait on me. I told him I wanted to order Jajangmyeon, but the old man didn't seem to understand me. Again, I told him slowly, "Jajangmyeon, please!" but he still couldn't understand me. At that time, an American old lady walked into the restaurant, and this time, I gave up on the noodle dish and ordered fried rice instead. This time, he understood me, and I went one step further to ask him for garlic. He said he only had garlic powder. Since I was dying for the taste of garlic, I agreed that would be fine. When he brought my order, I sprinkled a generous amount of garlic powder on the fried rice and devoured it. Only then did I feel my craving for garlic was satisfied, that I gained strength, and that my head became clearer. The taste of the fried rice I ate back then is still clearly imprinted in my memory.

RUSSIA'S WINDLESS COLD

Once, I had a business trip to Russia. Russia is famous for its biting cold, but it often feels less severe when you're actually there. This is an illusion, because of the lack of wind. You might not feel as cold, regardless of how low the temperature, if there's no wind. So, when I visited Russia, I didn't feel that cold. The temperature was definitely -20 degrees Celsius, but it didn't seem that cold, so I just went out and about everywhere. But gradually, I felt the cold creeping into my skin. This kind of cold penetrates deeply into the skin. You have to know that by the time you feel this, it's already too late. Normally, you recover from the cold's effects within an hour or two after returning to the hotel. However, even after returning to the hotel and going to bed, the cold lingered. The cold had already seeped deep into my skin. And even when I woke up, the cold hadn't gone away. At that moment, I was suddenly gripped by fear that something was wrong with my body. It was a moment when I realized the power of Russia's windless cold. Had I known this would happen, I would have been fully bundled up in layers before going out the previous day. Regret came too late, teaching me to never repeat the same mistake.

EXPERIENCE OF FLYING IN A SUPERSONIC AIRPLANE

During a business trip between America and Europe, I had the opportunity to fly on the Concorde, a supersonic plane. A supersonic airplane is one that flies at speeds ranging from Mach 2 to 3, more than twice as fast as a conventional airplane. I discovered this airplane while pressed for time, searching for the fastest way to reach my destination. Conventional airplanes take about 7 and a half hours to fly from New York to London, but a supersonic plane can cover the distance in just 3 and a half hours. The plane's seat dashboard displayed the plane's speed, such as Mach 1 or Mach 2, and people were excited to take pictures of it. I initially thought I was the only one inexperienced with such travel, but it turned out many others were also on a supersonic plane for the first time.

The seats on the plane were similar to regular airplanes, but the airfare was very expensive, costing about a thousand dollars more than a first-class ticket on a regular airplane. At the time, first class from New York to London was $3,300, but the supersonic plane ticket was $4,300. Nevertheless, time-strapped businessmen like me had no choice but to take this plane. I was able to have breakfast in London, fly on a supersonic plane to Washington to meet a client and have lunch. Then, I took the same plane back to London, arriving in time for dinner. I was amazed that the distance between London and Washington had become traversable in the same day.

Later, I heard heartbreaking news: On July 25, 2000, Air France's Concorde, a supersonic plane, suddenly caught fire and exploded shortly after takeoff from Paris Charles de Gaulle Airport, killing all 100 passengers and crew. The thought that it was the plane I had flown on gave me goosebumps. In the end, it's somewhat of a relief to know that supersonic airplanes have faded away due to cost issues and are no longer in use.

HOW I GOT HIT IN THE CALF BY A GOLF BALL

I remember the incident occurred at the Mauna Ocean Resort. I was playing the back nine of the 18-hole golf course when a golf ball suddenly struck my calf, hard. It was likely a ball struck with a 5-wood that hit my calf. However, I was so engrossed in the game that I didn't initially notice it. Then, the general affairs manager playing with me rushed over and asked if I was okay. Only then did I realize I had felt a dull impact on my calf, and when I looked around, I saw a golf ball about 2 meters away.

A typical golf bag contains about 13 to 14 clubs, depending on the player's selection. The driver is the longest club, capable of driving a ball 200 to 250 meters. The wood can send a ball flying 170 to 200 meters if hit well. I was probably hit by a ball someone struck with a 5-wood, indicating the blow was quite strong. The manager insisted that I should immediately go to the hospital for a thorough examination. I had no choice but to get tested. The area where the golf ball hit had turned black. However, the doctor assured me, "Your calf is so thick and strong that there's no problem with your bones. I'm envious that even at this age, you have such strong calves." Fortunately, I came away from the incident without any serious problems.

EPILOGUE

FOR THOSE PREPARING FOR THE SECOND HALF OF LIFE!

DO YOUR BEST IN YOUR FIELD!

If asked about the most important event in my life, the first thing that comes to mind is starting my own business. When I founded Ilsung, I had been working at KNOC for 19 years. It was a life of guaranteed stability, akin to a calm sea. However, as anyone with long-term employment knows, such work can lead to a repetitive routine. My experience was no different. In this context, when KNOC, a leading public enterprise, was taken over by the smaller Sunkyung, my loyalty to the company was shaken. It was then that I decided to start my own business.

What field would someone, who has been in the same job for 19 years, choose for starting a business? I chose a field where I could apply the professional skills I had honed over 19 years. In other words, I chose what I could do best, and it was the right decision. The underlying principle here is straightforward: If you choose a field that you are good in, you will likely excel, increasing your chances of success.

However, it's important to remember that even if you choose a field you are good in, success is not guaranteed. I worked hard to do my best by pouring my all into my business, determined that failure in a field I was proficient in would be unacceptable. When I first started my business, I was nervous for the first two months, as I had no orders coming in. Then, a 2 million won construction project came in, and I dedicated myself to completing it with excellence. I worked long hours, starting at 6:00 AM and not finishing until midnight. Thanks to this devotion, I was able to acquire detailed skills in the field. As an executive at KNOC, my opportunities to delve into the minutiae of the field were limited. However, my skills significantly improved as I immersed myself in the field's details. This experience enabled me to found Ilsung and grow it into a globally recognized company. In addition, I was even able to achieve the localization of petrochemical equipment technology.

Combining your best efforts with your expertise will inevitably maximize your chances of success, regardless of the challenges you face. Nowadays, we see many people jumping into entrepreneurship, and unfortunately, as the saying goes, most of them fail. I think the reason for this phenomenon is clear. Many retirees start businesses like chicken restaurants or cafes, but often lack professionalism due to it being their first venture. With limited expertise, even hard work cannot fully compensate, and your chances of success will inevitably diminish. Moreover, if you choose a field far from your expertise, your attachment to it will be less, leading to a diminished commitment and the mindset, "I can do this or something else." In contrast, there is an advantage in diving into work that allows you to utilize the expertise you have built over your entire life, as you will have a strong attachment to it. In summary, if you want to start a second business, the first important thing is to choose a field that you are good at, and the next important thing is to do your best in it, to the extent that you can even bet your life on it. When starting a business, you should never think that you can do this or something else if you fail in it.

A POSITIVE ATTITUDE MATTERS NO MATTER WHAT DIFFICULT SITUATION YOU ARE IN!

The second important event in my life would be when I entered college. At that time, my family was so impoverished that affording food was a challenge, let alone a college education. I was in a situation where I couldn't even dream of going to college. If I had chosen a different path back then, my life would have been different. However, I chose to move forward with a positive attitude and a singular goal: I was determined to forge ahead towards a global stage, envisioning a bright future. With no financial support from my parents, I overcame hardships and completed college by working as a live-in tutor for 6 years, including 2 years in ROTC, to cover tuition and living expenses.

Had I harbored negative thoughts about my circumstances at that time, I would never have overcome that difficult period in my life. I think I managed to surmount countless difficulties because I accepted my situation and environment as they were and moved forward with a positive attitude in everything.

If you live to be eighty years old and look back on your life, you realize that life is never a smooth ride. In life, you are bound to encounter many hardships. When difficulties arise, people usually fall into two categories: those who give in to the challenges and those who strive to overcome them. People who succumb to difficulties often fail to progress further, and in extreme cases, may find themselves mired in despair. It's important to remember that nature's challenges are not meant to defeat us. Difficulties are opportunities for growth. Therefore, when faced with challenges, it is vital to see them as growth opportunities and maintain a positive attitude to one day be someone who can overcome them.

No one likes to be put in a difficult situation, but I believe what truly matters is our attitude towards these difficulties. If difficulties are unavoidable, it's better to seek ways to overcome them. Positive thinking is the first step. As the saying goes, 'the ground hardens after the rain,' meaning challenges often lead to strength. By accepting that difficulties foster growth and striving to overcome them, you'll find that nature aids in your triumph. My life experience proves that.

THERE IS NO RETIREMENT IN LIFE!

The last thing I would like to say as a senior in life to those preparing for their second life is this: "There is no such word as retirement in today's world." Of course, there is a legal retirement age, and there is an age when one must leave their job, as no one can work indefinitely. However, we must keep in mind that there is no retirement in life. The reason why retirement is disappearing from life is because human lifespans are getting longer and society is developing day by day.

Did you know that the longest living person was said to be Li Chengyuan, who allegedly lived 256 years in Sichuan Province, China? He was born in 1677 AD and died in May 1933, making him the world's longest-living person, according to the claims. He was acclaimed as the greatest medical scientist of his era, specializing in medicinal herbs, and is reputed to have given university lectures even at 200 years old. In 1930, just before his death, he was featured in the New York Times. During his lifetime, he allegedly had 24 wives and as many as 200 children.

While it's an incredible story, the human lifespan is indeed extending, with many now approaching 100 years. In this era, retiring at the age of sixty may no longer be the norm. In the past, retiring at age 60 and beginning a quieter phase of life was seen as virtuous, but now, it's seen as equally virtuous to work throughout life in a field where you can contribute to the world and pursue lifelong learning. Therefore, to live wisely in this new era, it's essential to actively prepare for a second career, as working is beneficial for your health and also a way to contribute to society. This need arises due to the rapid changes brought about by the digital and AI era. By preparing for the future, you'll find opportunities to work, regardless of age. This is why I continue to study and never be without a book even at this age. My goal is to contribute to society for as long as I live.

A SECOND LIFE BEGINS WITH EFFORTS TO STAY IN GOOD SHAPE

It must be emphasized that the cornerstone of living a second life is maintaining good health. Everyone knows the importance of health without needing further explanation. Maintaining good health is akin to nurturing a flower; just like a flower that withers without care, your health will deteriorate if neglected. As we age, it becomes more important to exert extra effort in maintaining our health, as the human body, like machinery, tends to wear down over time. I have recognized this fact since my youth and have actively engaged in sports I enjoy, such as tennis, badminton, golf, swimming, and skiing. Most notably, I continue to hike barefoot and even take cold baths at my age, which greatly benefits my health. Specifically, walking barefoot on the ground, known as 'earthing,' is highly beneficial to health, and I hope more people will practice it.

People preparing for a second life should avoid the mindset that 'I have worked hard so far, so I will rest after retirement.' Such an attitude does not guarantee health and happiness in old age. This insight is based on my own experience, so you can rely on its validity. Instead, choose to say, 'I have worked hard until now, so I will work happily in my old age.' Adopting this mindset will pave the way to health and happiness in your second life.

BIO OF THE AUTHOR, CHANG SEIL

Education

Feb. 1958	Graduated from Gyeongbuk High School
Feb. 1963	Graduated from Seoul National University College of Engineering, Department of Electrical Engineering

Major Career

Mar. 1963 - Mar. 1965	Discharged as army second lieutenant commission (ROTC 1st class)
May. 1965 - Dec. 1983	Korea National Oil Corporation (currently, SK E&P Company) Public Affairs, Engineering & Maintenance Department Manager
Jan. 1984 - Oct. 1999	President of Ilsung Industries
Nov. 1999 - May 2000	CEO of Ilsung Co., Ltd.
Jun. 2000 - Jan. 2007	CEO and Chairman of Ilsung Engineering Co., Ltd.
Jan. 2007 - Nov. 2016	Chairman of Ilsung Co., Ltd.
Dec. 2016 - present	Honorary Chairman of Ilsung Hisco Co., Ltd.

Trainings

Jun. 28, 1994	Completed the 29th CEO course at the Federation of Korean Industries International Business Institute
Aug. 20, 1997	Completed the 2nd Federation of Korean Industries Information Strategy CEO Course
Sep. 25, 1997	Completed Advanced Leadership Program (Harris Manchester College, University of Oxford)
Jul. 3, 1999	Completed the 1st Global Business School Executive Program of the Federation of Korean Industries
Aug. 6, 1999	Completed Building Competitive Advantage Through Operations course (Havard University)
Dec. 18, 2001	Received an honorary doctorate in business administration from Lincoln University
Jun. 29, 2007	Completed Shanghai Jiaotong University (China) Advanced Accounting SMBA Course (7th class)
Jul. 18, 2022	Completed Techno CEO Course (11th class) at Ulsan University Graduate School of Industry

Social Activities

Apr. 1998 - 2011	Korean Red Cross national representative
Jan. 2000 - Apr. 2010	President of Ulsan Tennis Association
Jun. 2000 - 2011	Director of Seoul National University Alumni Association
Jan. 2000 - Jan. 2014	Vice Chairman of Ulsan-Yangsan Regional Council, Crime Prevention Committee, Ministry of Justice

Mar. 2000 - 2011	Director of the Korea International Trade Association and Honorary Chairman of the Ulsan Chamber of Commerce and Industry
Feb. 2001 - 2011	Director, International Management Institute, Federation of Korean Industries
Jan. 2009 - 2014	Vice Chairman of Ulsan Chamber of Commerce and Industry
Jan. 2010 - 2011	First Chairman of the Plant Equipment Industry Council

Accolades

Mar. 4, 1991	Commendation for faithful tax payment (Director of the National Tax Service)
Mar. 29, 1991	Commerce and Industry Grand Prize - Management Category (Ulsan Chamber of Commerce and Industry)
Jun. 29, 1991	The 1st Gyeongnam Industrial Peace Grand Prize
Dec. 27, 1991	Industrial Peace Industrial Service Award (President Roh Tae-woo)
Oct. 17, 1992	Award for being an excellent company for promotion of skills (Ministry of Labor)
Nov. 30, 1993	Million Dollar Export Tower (President Kim Young-sam)
Jul. 1, 1994	Marketing Innovation Award (Korea Productivity Center)
Jul. 1, 1994	Designation as an excellent company for productivity improvement (government)
Mar. 3, 1995	Citation for faithful performance of tax payment obligations (Busan Regional Tax Office)

May 12, 1995	National Exemplary Small Business Award (President Kim Young-sam)
Nov. 29, 1995	Proud New Korean Award (President Kim Young-sam)
Aug. 4, 1996	'96 Proud Gyeongnam Province Citizen Award (South Gyeongsang Province Governor)
Sep. 12, 1996	Award for being an excellent company for skills promotion - twice in a row (Ministry of Labor)
Aug. 21, 1997	Business Executive Grand Prize (National Federation of Korean Industries)
Oct. 1, 1997	Ulsan Metropolitan City Industrial Peace Award - Gold Prize (Ulsan Metropolitan City)
Mar. 3, 1998	Citation for faithful performance of tax payment obligations (National Tax Service)
Nov. 30, 1998	Ten Million Dollar Export Tower (President Kim Dae-jung)
Nov. 30, 1999	$30 Million Export Tower (President Kim Dae-jung)
Dec. 13, 1999	'99 CEO Grand Prize (National Federation of Industries)
Feb. 22, 2001	Business Executive Grand Prize - Global Business Leadership Award (Federation of Korean Industries - International Business Institute)
Nov. 1, 2001	Award for being an excellent company for vocational competency development (Prime Minister)
Nov. 30, 2006	Seventy Million Dollar Export Tower (President Roh Moo-hyun)

Dec. 2, 2008	100 Million Dollar Export Tower (President Lee Myung-bak)
Dec. 16, 2009	Trader of the Year Award for Glorifying Korea (Korea International Trade Association)
Nov. 30, 2010	Gold Tower Order of Industrial Service Merit (President Lee Myung-bak)
May. 16, 2011	5/16 National Award, Industrial Category Grand Prize (5/16 National Award)

SMALL DETAILS MAKE
A BIG DIFFERENCE

초판 1쇄 인쇄 _ 2024년 3월 20일
초판 1쇄 발행 _ 2024년 3월 25일

지은이 _ 장세일

펴낸곳 _ 바이북스
펴낸이 _ 윤옥초
책임편집 _ 김태윤
책임디자인 _ 이민영

ISBN _ 979-11-5877-372-4 03190

등록 _ 2005. 7. 12 | 제 313-2005-000148호

서울시 영등포구 선유로49길 23 아이에스비즈타워2차 1005호
편집 02)333-0812 | 마케팅 02)333-9918 | 팩스 02)333-9960
이메일 bybooks85@gmail.com
블로그 https://blog.naver.com/bybooks85

책값은 뒤표지에 있습니다.

책으로 아름다운 세상을 만듭니다. — 바이북스

미래를 함께 꿈꿀 작가님의 참신한 아이디어나 원고를 기다립니다.
이메일로 접수된 원고는 검토 후 연락드리겠습니다.